A Basic Dictionary of Bible People

Julien Chilcott-Monk spent two years in the Royal Marines School of Music, and four years at Kelham Theological College, where he learnt, inter alia, to mimic – doubtless rather imperfectly – the professed brethren of the Society of the Sacred Mission. He has since worked for many years in law and litigation. His last book, an Advent title, *Come, Lord Jesus!*, was written jointly with the Bishop of Gibraltar and published by Canterbury Press in 2002.

Other titles in the Basic Dictionary series published by
Canterbury Press

A Basic Bible Dictionary
A Basic Catholic Dictionary
A Basic Church Dictionary
A Basic Dictionary of Saints

A Basic Dictionary of Bible People

Julien Chilcott-Monk

CANTERBURY
PRESS
Norwich

First published in 2004 by the Canterbury Press Norwich
(a publishing imprint of Hymns Ancient &
Modern Limited, a registered charity)
St Mary's Works, St Mary's Plain
Norwich, Norfolk, NR3 3BH

www.scm-canterburypress.co.uk

Maps by John Flower

British Library Cataloguing in Publication data
A catalogue record for this book is available
from the British Library

ISBN 1-85311-567-3

Typeset by Regent Typesetting, London
Printed and bound in Great Britain by
Bookmarque, Croydon, Surrey

Contents

List of Diagrams

For Susan
With apologies for not mentioning Isaiah's son,
Maher-shalal-hash-baz, within!

My thanks are due to Fiona Bolton for tackling the Index, and for making sense of my parallel histories so ably. JCM

Introduction

This book is not called a 'basic' dictionary simply to ensure that the reader's expectations of it are not too high! The book is part of a series of dictionaries whose aim is to provide a platform of information and the basis for further enquiry. In the case of this book, it is hoped that the reader will be able to approach the text of the Bible armed with a little more knowledge about the background and circumstances of the significant and important groups of people encountered in the Old and New Testaments.

Although individuals are sometimes listed under the principal entry – disciples, priests, prophets etc. – the reader will not find in this book all individuals named in the Bible, for example, most of those contained in Romans 16.23 and in Acts 20.1–6. Indeed, there are many groups – for example, some of the clans and families named in Numbers 26 and in 1 Chronicles 2.53–55, and the almost innumerable '-ites' mentioned in 2 Samuel 23.24 – not to be found, on account of the fact that they rarely, if ever, feature again in the Bible. And I have not included a rather important group – that of the angels. They cannot be dealt with cursorily. Indeed, can they be thought of as Bible *people?* The divine will is obviously carried out and revealed from time to time through the agency of men acting as God's messengers or, perhaps, by purely spiritual beings assuming the appearance of men, or assuming an identity acceptable to the recipient of the message. The wings of the angels are, for the most part (as far as we can tell), devices and metaphors employed in literature, painting and sculpture, to make the point of the immediacy and omniscience of God, and of the speed of the transmission of his word and message.

Out of further study of the Bible comes a dawning of how marvellous is the manner in which God reveals himself to mankind. The first understanding to emerge was that he was a personal God, but one of a number, albeit a superior God; then, that he was the only God, and, furthermore, not only the God of Israel but also the God of all nations. Slowly but surely the picture of the mystery that is God emerges by means of the action of God through history and through the understanding of the prophets, who, rather perhaps like poets, often revealed more than they themselves knew. This picture in any stage of its developing image has always challenged mankind. As Jesus himself tells the disciples, the whole truth is too much to take in all at once, but 'when the Spirit of truth comes, he will guide you into all the truth' (John 16.13). Only after Jesus' resurrection and ascension did the Early Church begin to see that the cumulative effect of the prophets' messianic hope throughout the ages, pointed clearly to Jesus, the embodiment of God's love, who is the full and perfect revelation of the nature of God.

Who were the prophets? When were they active? Do all the Gospels agree on the names of the disciples? Who was related to whom? Did Jesus have brothers? Who were the women at the cross? Why do the Gospels not agree upon who they were? Who were the writers of the Bible? There are answers and suggestions as to answers to these questions in order to nudge the reader back to the text of the Bible and, perhaps, to further study. The reader will find charts, family trees and maps to assist in unravelling some of the confusions and difficulties encountered in the Old and New Testaments, together with ample cross-references to allow connections to be made that otherwise, perhaps, might not be made.

In this book all quotations are taken from the *New Revised Standard Version*, largely because it is, on the whole, an accurate translation and commonly in use in schools and colleges. Nevertheless, it is of great benefit to any student of the Bible to consult and study as many translations as possible – from the Wycliffe to the Authorized Version; from Tyndale to the Douay Version; from the Revised Version to the New English Version, and so on.

Julien Chilcott-Monk

Alphabetical Listing of Groups and Individuals

This listing includes individuals examined in the text and refers the reader to the principal entries in which their names occur.

Aaron *see* Priests and High Priests and Principal People of the Exodus, the Wilderness and Entry into Canaan.

Aaronites

Abdon *see* Judges

Abiathar *see* Priests and High Priests

Abijam *see* Kings of the Kingdom of Judah

Abimelech *see* Kings of Other Lands

Abinadab *see* Priests and High Priests

Abraham *see* Patriarchs

Abram *see* entries for Abraham

Achish *see* Kings of Other Lands

Adam *see* Characters of the Creation and Great Flood Stories

Adoni-bezek *see* Kings of Other Lands

Adoni-zedek *see* Kings of Other Lands

Adullamites

Aeneus *see* People of the Acts of the Apostles

Agag *see* Kings of Other Lands

Ahab *see* Kings of the Kingdom of Israel

Ahasuerus *see* Kings of Other Lands

Ahaz *see* Kings of the Kingdom of Judah

Ahaziah (son of Ahab) *see* Kings of the Kingdom of Israel

Ahaziah (son of Jehoram) *see* Kings of the Kingdom of Judah

Ahijah *see* Prophets of the Old Testament

Ahimelech *see* Priests and High Priests

Ahmose *see* Kings of Other Lands

Akkadians

Alexander Janneus *see* Priests and High Priests

Alexandrians

Amaziah *see* Kings of the Kingdom of Judah

Amalekites

Alphabetical Listing of Groups and Individuals

Ammonites
Amon *see* Kings of the
  Kingdom of Judah
Amorites
Amos *see* Prophets of the Old
  Testament
Amraphel *see* Kings of Other
  Lands
Ananias *see* People of the Acts
  of the Apostles
Ananias (priest) *see* Priests
  and High Priests
Ancestors of King David
Ancestors of King Saul
Andrew *see* Disciples of Jesus
  and Friends, Relations and
  Acquaintances of Jesus
Anna *see* Friends, Relations
  and Acquaintances of Jesus
Annas *see* Priests and High
  Priests
Antaxerxes I *see* Kings of
  Other Lands
Apollos *see* People of the Acts
  of the Apostles
Apostles
Aquila and Priscilla *see* People
  of the Acts of the Apostles
Arameans
Archelaus *see* Herods
Archippus *see* People of the
  Letters of the New
  Testament
Arioch *see* Kings of Other Lands
Aristarchus *see* People of the
  Acts of the Apostles
Arkites
Arvadites
Asa *see* Kings of the Kingdom
  of Judah
Ashdodites
Asher, tribe of
Ashur-banipal *see* Kings of
  Other Lands

Assyrians
Athaliah *see* Kings of the
  Kingdom of Judah
Azariah (Uzziah) *see* Kings of
  the Kingdom of Judah

Baasha *see* Kings of the
  Kingdom of Israel
Babylonians
Balak *see* Kings of Other Lands
Bar-Jesus *see* People of the
  Acts of the Apostles
Barnabas *see* People of the
  Acts of the Apostles
Bartholomew *see* Friends,
  Relations and Acquaintances
  of Jesus – Nathanael and
  Disciples of Jesus –
  Nathanael Bartholomew
Bartimaeus *see* Friends,
  Relations and Acquaintances
  of Jesus
Baruch (Baruch/The Letter
  of Jeremiah) *see* Writers of
  the Old Testament
Belshazzar *see* Kings of Other
  Lands
Ben-hadad I *see* Kings of Other
  Lands
Ben-hadad II *see* Kings of
  Other Lands
Benjamin, Tribe of
Bilhah *see* Diagram 3. Children
  of Israel
Brothers of Jesus

Cain and Abel, sons of Adam
  and Eve *see* Characters of
  the Creation and Great Flood
  stories
Caleb *see* Principal People of
  the Exodus, the Wilderness
  and Entry into Canaan
Canaanites
Candace *see* Kings of Other
  Lands

Carites
Cephas see Friends, Relations
and Acquaintances of Jesus
Chaldeans
Characters of the Creation
and Great Flood Stories
Chedorlaomer see Kings of
Other Lands
Children of Israel
Chosen People
Christians
1 and 2 Chronicles see Writers
of the Old Testament
Cleopas see Friends, Relations
and Acquaintances of Jesus
Clopas see Friends, Relations
and Acquaintances of Jesus
Colossians
Colossians, Letter to see Letter
Writers of the New Testament
Corinthians
Corinthians, First Letter to see
Letter Writers of the New
Testament
Corinthians, Second Letter to
see Letter Writers of the New
Testament
Cornelius see People of the
Acts of the Apostles
Crispus see People of the Acts
of the Apostles
Cushites
Cyrus the Great see Kings of
Other Lands

Damaris see People of the Acts
of the Apostles
Dan, tribe of
Daniel see Prophets of the Old
Testament
Darius I see Kings of Other
Lands
David see Kings of the United
Kingdom of Israel

Deacons, Seven
Debir see Kings of Other
Lands
Deborah see Judges and
Prophets of the Old
Testament
Demas see People of the
Letters of the New
Testament
Deuteronomy see Writers of
the Old Testament
Diaspora
Dionysius see People of the
Acts of the Apostles
Disciples of Jesus
Disciples of John the Baptist
Dorcas see People of the Acts
of the Apostles

Ecclesiastes see Writers of the
Old Testament
Edomites
Eglon see Kings of Other
Lands
Egyptians
Ehud see Judges
Elah see Kings of the Kingdom
of Israel
Elamites
Eleazer see Priests and High
Priests
Eli see Judges, Priests and
High Priests and Prophets of
the Old Testament
Elijah see Prophets of the Old
Testament
Elisha see Prophets of the Old
Testament
Elizabeth see Friends,
Relations and Acquaintances
of Jesus
Elon see Judges
Epaphras see People of the
Letters of the New Testament

Alphabetical Listing of Groups and Individuals

Writers of the New
Testament
Hellenists
Herod Agrippa I *see* Herods
Herod Agrippa II *see* Herods
Herod Antipas *see* Herods
Herod Philip *see* Herods
Herod the Great *see* Herods
Herodians
Herods
Hezekiah *see* Kings of the
Kingdom of Judah
Hilkiah *see* Priests and High
Priests
Hiram *see* Kings of Other
Lands
Hittites
Hivites
Hoham *see* Kings of Other
Lands
Holy Family
Horam *see* Kings of Other
Lands
Horites
Hosea *see* Prophets of the Old
Testament
Hoshea *see* Kings of the
Kingdom of Israel
Hurrians
Hyksos
Hyrcanus *see* Priests and High
Priests

Ibzan *see* Judges
Idumeans
Isaac *see* Patriarchs
Isaiah *see* Prophets of the Old
Testament
Ishbaal (Ish-bosheth) *see* Kings
of the United Kingdom of
Israel
Ishmaelites
Israel (Jacob) *see* Children of
Israel

Israel, Tribes of
Israelites
Issachar, Tribe of
Ithamar *see* Priests and High
Priests
Ithrites

Jabin *see* Kings of Other Lands
Jacob *see* Patriarchs
Jair *see* Judges
Jairus *see* Friends, Relations
and Acquaintances of Jesus
James I 'the Great' (apostle)
see Disciples of Jesus,
Friends, Relations and
Acquaintances of Jesus and ·
People of the Acts of the
Apostles
James II (apostle) *see* Disciples
of Jesus and Friends,·
Relations and Acquaintances
of Jesus
James III 'the Less' *see*
Friends, Relations and
Acquaintances of Jesus,
People of the Acts of the
Apostles and Letter Writers
of the New Testament
James, Letter of *see* Letter
Writers of the New
Testament
James, Principal Individuals
Named
Japhia *see* Kings of Other
Lands
Jason *see* People of the Acts of
the Apostles
Jebusites
Jehoahaz (son of Jehu) *see*
Kings of the Kingdom of
Israel
Jehoahaz (son of Josiah) *see*
Kings of the Kingdom of
· Judah

Alphabetical Listing of Groups and Individuals

Jehoiachin *see* Kings of the
Kingdom of Judah
Jehoiakim (Eliakim) *see* Kings
of the Kingdom of Judah
Jehoiada *see* Priests and High
Priests
Jehoram (Joram) (son of
Ahab) *see* Kings of the
Kingdom of Israel
Jehoram (Joram) (son of
Jehoshaphat) *see* Kings of
the Kingdom of Judah
Jehoshaphat *see* Kings of the
Kingdom of Judah
Jehu *see* Kings of the Kingdom
of Israel
Jephthah *see* Judges
Jerahmeelites
Jeremiah *see* Prophets of the
Old Testament
Jeroboam *see* Kings of the
Kingdom of Israel
Jeroboam II *see* Kings of the
Kingdom of Israel
Jeshua *see* Priests and High
Priests
Jesus *see* Family of Jesus
Jews
Joanna *see* Friends, Relations
and Acquaintances of Jesus
Joash (Jehoash) *see* Kings of
the Kingdom of Judah
Joash (Jehoash) (son of
Jehoahaz) *see* Kings of the
Kingdom of Israel
Job *see* Writers of the Old
Testament
Jobab (King of Edom) *see*
Kings of Other Lands
Jobab (King of Madon) *see*
Kings of Other Lands
Joel *see* Prophets of the Old
Testament
John (apostle) *see* Disciples of

Jesus, Friends, Relations
and Acquaintances of Jesus
and People of the Acts of the
Apostles
John (evangelist) *see*
Evangelists and Letter Writers
of the New Testament,
John (father of Andrew and
Simon Peter) *see* Friends,
Relations and Acquaintances
of Jesus
John (John Mark) *see* People
of the Acts of the Apostles
and entries for Mark
(evangelist)
John the Baptist *see* Friends,
Relations and Acquaintances
of Jesus and Prophets of the
Old Testament
John the Divine *see* Writers of
the New Testament –
Revelation
John, Three Letters of *see*
Letter Writers of the New
Testament
Jonah *see* Prophets of the Old
Testament
Jonathan *see* Priests and High
Priests
Joseph (Joses) *see* Friends,
Relations and Acquaintances
of Jesus
Joseph of Arimathea *see*
Friends, Relations and
Acquaintances of Jesus
Joseph Barsabbas *see* Friends,
Relations and Acquaintances
of Jesus
Joseph, Guardian of Jesus *see*
Friends, Relations and
Acquaintances of Jesus
Joseph, Son of Jacob
Joseph, Principal Individuals
Named

Alphabetical Listing of Groups and Individuals

Joseph, tribe of

Joshua *see* Principal People of the Exodus, the Wilderness and Entry into Canaan

Joshua *see* Writers of the Old Testament

Josiah *see* Kings of the Kingdom of Judah

Jotham *see* Kings of the Kingdom of Judah

Judah, tribe of

Judas (Jude) *see* Friends, Relations and Acquaintances of Jesus and Letter Writers of the New Testament – Jude

Judas (not Iscariot) *see* Disciples of Jesus and Friends, Relations and Acquaintances of Jesus

Judas Barsabbas *see* People of the Acts of the Apostles

Judas Iscariot *see* Disciples of Jesus and Friends, Relations and Acquaintances of Jesus

Judas Maccabeus *see* Hasmoneans and Maccabees

Judas, Principal Individuals Named

Jude *see* entries for Judas (Jude)

Jude, Letter of *see* Letter Writers of the New Testament

Judges

Judges *see* Writers of the Old Testament

Judith *see* Writers of the Old Testament

Kenites

Kenizzites

1 and 2 Kings (also known as 3 and 4 Kings) *see* Writers of the Old Testament

Kings of Other Lands

Kings of the Kingdom of Israel

Kings of the Kingdom of Judah

Kings of the United Kingdom of Israel

Korahites

Lamentations *see* Writers of the Old Testament

Lazarus *see* Friends, Relations and Acquaintances of Jesus

Leah *see* Diagram 3. Children of Israel

Letter Writers of the New Testament

Levi (Matthew) *see* Friends, Relations and Acquaintances of Jesus and Disciples of Jesus – Matthew

Levi, Tribe of

Leviticus *see* Writers of the Old Testament

Luke (evangelist) *see* Evangelists

Maacathites

Maccabees

1 and 2 Maccabees *see* Writers of the Old Testament

3 and 4 Maccabees *see* Writers of the Old Testament

Malachai *see* Prophets of the Old Testament

Manasseh *see* Kings of the Kingdom of Judah

Manasseh, Tribe of

Maonites

Mark (evangelist) *see* Evangelists and People of the Acts of the Apostles – John

Martha *see* Friends, Relations and Acquaintances of Jesus

Martyrs of the Early Church

Mary of Bethany *see* Friends, Relations and Acquaintances of Jesus

7

Alphabetical Listing of Groups and Individuals

Mary (mother of John Mark)
see People of the Acts of the
Apostles

Mary Magdalene see Friends,
Relations and Acquaintances
of Jesus

Mary, Mother of Jesus see
Friends, Relations and
Acquaintances of Jesus

Mary, Principal Individuals
Named

Mary, Wife of Clopas see
Friends, Relations and
Acquaintances of Jesus

Matthew (apostle) see
Disciples of Jesus, and
Friends, Relations and
Acquaintances of Jesus

Matthew (evangelist) see
Evangelists

Matthias see Friends, Relations
and Acquaintances of Jesus
and People of the Acts of the
Apostles

Medes

Melchizedek see Priests and
High Priests

Menahem see Kings of the
Kingdom of Israel

Meremoth see Priests and
High Priests

Merodach-baladan see Kings
of Other Lands

Mesha see Kings of Other
Lands

Micah see Prophets of the Old
Testament

Micaiah see Prophets of the
Old Testament

Midianites

Miriam see Principal People
of the Exodus, the
Wilderness and Entry
into Canaan

Mitannians

Moabites

Moses see Principal People of
the Exodus, the Wilderness
and Entry into Canaan

Nabateans

Nabonidus see Kings of Other
Lands

Nabopolassar see Kings of
Other Lands

Nadab see Kings of the
Kingdom of Israel

Nahash see Kings of Other
Lands

Nahum see Prophets of the
Old Testament

Naphtali, Tribe of

Nathan see Prophets of the Old
Testament

Nathanael Bartholomew see
Disciples of Jesus, and
Friends, Relations and
Acquaintances of Jesus

Nebuchadnezzer
(Nebuchadrezzer) see Kings
of Other Lands

Neco see Kings of Other Lands

Nehemiah see Writers of the
Old Testament – Ezra and
Nehemiah

Netophathites

Nicodemus see Friends,
Relations and Acquaintances
of Jesus

Noah see Characters of the
Creation and Great Flood
stories

Nomads and Semi-Nomads

Nubians

Numbers see Writers of the
Old Testament

Obadiah see Prophets of the
Old Testament

Og *see* Kings of Other Lands
Omri *see* Kings of the
   Kingdom of Israel
Onesimus *see* People of the
   Letters of the New
   Testament
Othniel *see* Judges

Patriarchs
Paul (Saul) *see* Letter Writers
   of the New Testament, and
   People of the Acts of the
   Apostles
Pekah *see* Kings of the
   Kingdom of Israel
Pekahiah *see* Kings of
   the Kingdom of
   Israel
People of the Acts of the
   Apostles
People of the Babylonian
   Captivity and Return
People of the Letters of the
   New Testament (not
   mentioned in Acts)
Perezites
Perizzites
Persians
Peter, First Letter of *see* Letter
   Writers of the New
   Testament
Peter, Second Letter of *see*
   Letter Writers of the New
   Testament
Peter (Simon Peter) *see*
   Disciples of Jesus, Friends,
   Relations and Acquaintances
   of Jesus, Letter Writers of the
   New Testament and People
   of the Acts of the Apostles
Pharaohs
Pharisees
Philemon *see* People of the
   Letters of the New Testament

Philemon, Letter to *see* Letter
   Writers of the New
   Testament
Philip *see* Disciples of Jesus
   and Friends, Relations and
   Acquaintances of Jesus
Philip (deacon) *see* People of
   the Acts of the Apostles
Philip the Tetrarch *see* Herods
Philippians
Philippians, Letter to *see* Letter
   Writers of the New
   Testament
Philistines
Phineas *see* Priests and High
   Priests
Phoenicians
Piram *see* Kings of Other
   Lands
Pirathonites
Prayer of Manasseh *see*
   Writers of the Old Testament
Priests and High Priests
Principal People of the Exodus,
   the Wilderness and Entry
   into Canaan
Priscilla *see* People of the Acts
   of the Apostles
Prophets of the Old Testament
Proverbs *see* Writers of the Old
   Testament
Psalms *see* Writers of the Old
   Testament
Ptolemys
Publius *see* People of the Acts
   of the Apostles
Pul *see* Kings of Other Lands

Rabbis
Rachel *see* Diagram 3:
   Children of Israel
Rameses II *see* Kings of Other
   Lands
Rebekah *see* Patriarchs – Isaac

Alphabetical Listing of Groups and Individuals

Alphabetical Listing of Groups and Individuals

Relations and Acquaintances
of Jesus

Simon the Pharisee *see*
Friends, Relations and
Acquaintances of Jesus

Simon the Zealot (or the
Canaanite) *see* Disciples of
Jesus and Friends, Relations
and Acquaintances of Jesus

Simon *see* Friends, Relations
and Acquaintances of Jesus

Simon, Principal Individuals
Named

Sinites

Sirach (Ecclesiasticus) *see*
Writers of the Old Testament

Sodomites

Solomon *see* Kings of the
United Kingdom of Israel

Song of Solomon (Song of
Songs/Canticle of Canticles)
see Writers of the Old
Testament

Sosthenes *see* Letter Writers of
the New Testament and
People of the Letters of the
New Testament

Sosthenes (official) *see* People
of the Acts of the Apostles

Stephen *see* People of the Acts
of the Apostles

Stoics *see* Epicureans and
Stoics

Sumerians

Susanna *see* Friends, Relations
and Acquaintances of Jesus

Syrians

Tabitha *see* People of the Acts
of the Apostles

Ten Tribes of Israel or Lost
Tribes of Israel

Thaddeus *see* Friends,
Relations and Acquaintances

of Jesus – Judas (not Iscariot)

Thessalonians

Thessalonians, First Letter to
see Letter Writers of the New
Testament

Thessalonians, Sceond Letter
to *see* Letter Writers of the
New Testament

Thomas *see* Disciples of Jesus
and Friends, Relations and
Acquaintances of Jesus

Tibni and Omri *see* Kings of the
kingdom of Israel

Tiglath-pileser III *see* Kings of
Other Lands

Timothy *see* People of the Acts
of the Apostles

Timothy, First and Second
Letters to, and Titus, Letter to
see Letter Writers of the New
Testament

Titus *see* People of the Letters
of the New Testament

Tobit (Tobias) *see* Writers of
the Old Testament

Tola *see* Judges

Tou *see* Kings of Other Lands

Twelve

Twelve Tribes of Israel

Tychicus *see* People of the Acts
of the Apostles

Wisdom of Solomon (The Book
of Wisdom) *see* Writers of the
Old Testasment

Wise Men of the Birth of Jesus

Women at the Cross of Jesus
and at the Tomb

Writers of the New Testament

Writers of the Old Testament

Zacchaeus *see* Friends,
Relations and Acquaintances
of Jesus

11

Alphabetical Listing of Groups and Individuals

A Basic Dictionary of Bible People

Aaronites

The descendants of Aaron and the principal priestly family of Israel. 'Then bring near to you your brother Aaron, and his sons with him, from among the Israelites, to serve me as priests – Aaron and Aaron's sons, Nadab and Abihu, Eleazar and Ithamar' (Exodus 28.1). Aaron was high priest, elder brother of Moses and of the tribe of Levi. 'Amram married Jochebed his father's sister and she bore him Aaron and Moses, and the length of Amram's life was one hundred and thirty-seven years' (Exodus 6.20). The two brothers were responsible for the planning and strategy of the Exodus from Egypt, and for the leadership of the Israelites during their time in the wilderness. 'It was this same Aaron and Moses to whom the Lord said, "Bring the Israelites out of the land of Egypt, company by company" (Exodus 6.26). The family tree of the tribe of Levi given in Exodus 6 is probably a 'telescoped' account of the generations between the settling in Egypt and the Exodus. That period was believed by the writers of Exodus to be over four hundred years. 'The time that the Israelites lived in Egypt was four hundred and thirty years' (Exodus 12.40). It is, of course, not always possible to rely on the accuracy of such figures without external and archaeological evidence in support, and so most of the argument among biblical scholars and historians is concerned with trying to establish the date of the descent into Egypt by the Children of Israel and the date of the Exodus.
(see *Egyptians and Kings of Other Lands – Ahmose, Rameses II and Seti I*)

Diagrams
Children of Israel (3)
Tree of the Tribe of Levi (4)
Broad Parallel Histories (16, 17)

Adullamites

The inhabitants of Adullam, south west of Bethlehem, where part of King David's army was stationed (1 Chronicles 11.15).

Akkadians

Under Sargon the Akkadians defeated the Sumerians in *c.* 2300 BC and replaced the Sumerian Empire with their own, which lasted until about 2180 BC when the bellicose Gutians came from the Caucasus mountains.
(see *Sumerians*)

13

Alexandrians

The inhabitants of the empire of Alexander the Great and, perhaps more specifically, the inhabitants of Alexandria in Egypt.
(see *Greeks, Grecians and Hellenists*)

Amalekites

The descendants of Amalek, the grandson of Esau. 'Timna was a concubine of Eliphaz, Esau's son; she bore Amalek to Elipha' (Genesis 36.12). They were a semi-nomadic people who had moved westwards from Edom and settled in the land between Egypt and Canaan hindering the Israelites in their Exodus from Egypt and in their progress from the wilderness of Sinai towards the Promised Land. 'Then Amalek came and fought with Israel at Rephidim. Moses said to Joshua, "Choose some men for us and go out; fight with Amalek . . ." So Joshua did as Moses told him, and fought with Amalek . . . And Joshua defeated Amalek and his people with the sword . . . And Moses . . . said ". . . The Lord will have war with Amalek from generation to generation"' (Exodus 17.8–16).They continued variously to annoy, harry and threaten the Israelites to the time of King Saul and King David. Towards the end of his reign, Saul defeated the Amalekites in a great battle. However, he incurred Samuel's displeasure by sparing the life of King Agag, king of the Amalekites. This error of judgement precipitated Saul's decline. 'Saul defeated the Amalekites from Havilah as far as Shur, which is east of Egypt. He took King Agag of the Amalekites alive, but utterly destroyed all the people with the edge of the sword. Saul and his people spared Agag' (1 Samuel 15.7–9a). David is later credited with the demise of the Amalekites: 'these also King David dedicated to the Lord, together with the silver and gold that he dedicated from all the nations he subdued, from Edom, Moab, the Ammonites, the Philistines, Amalek, and from the spoil of King Hadadezer son of Rehob of Zobah' (2 Samuel 8.11, 12).

Diagrams
Descent of Abraham (1)
Family of Abraham (2)
Map of Canaan (6)

Ammonites

The Ammonites were descendants of Lot's son Ben-ammi; a sedentary people who settled the land east of Jordan. They entered into an alliance against Israel with the Amalekites and the Moabites. 'The Israelites again did what was evil in the sight of the Lord; and the Lord strengthened King Eglon of Moab against Israel, because they had done what was evil in the sight of the Lord. In alliance with the Ammonites and the Amalekites, he went and defeated Israel; and they took possession of the city of palms' (Judges 3.12, 13). The Amalekites were subdued by Jephthah, and finally conquered by King David. 'So Jephthah crossed over to the Ammonites to fight against them; and the Lord gave them into his hand. He inflicted a massive defeat on them from Aroer to the neighbourhood of Minith, twenty towns, and as far as Abel-ker-amim. So the Ammonites were subdued before the people of Israel' (Judges 11.32,33) '. . . these also King David dedicated to the Lord together with the silver and gold that he dedicated from all the nations he subdued, from Edom, Moab, the Ammonites, the Philistines, Amalek, and from the spoil of King Hadadezer son of Rehob of Zobah' (2 Samuel 8.11, 12).

Diagrams
Family of Abraham (2)
Map of Canaan (6)

Amorites

In the fourth and third millennia BC, the Sumerians and Akkadians had alternately controlled Mesopotamia until the Elamites and others brought instability from beyond the river Tigris, and it was into this bewilderment that the Amorites – a Semitic and semi-nomadic people – spread from the Arabian Desert at the beginning of the second millennium BC. With incredible speed and determination they secured Mesopotamia and established the first Babylonian Empire and, by the time of the last king, Hammurabi, 1728–1686 BC, it embraced the kingdom of Mari, a city on the Euphrates, roughly midway between Haran and Babylon, and it was here that many thousands of clay tablets were found not long before the Second World War. These tablets were records of dealings with other Amoritic states of Hammurabi's empire and, most significantly, feature names familiar to us such as David and Benjamin. Furthermore, there is also mention of the 'Apiru' – i.e. the Hebrews.

The migration of Abraham's family from Ur to Haran and into Canaan may well have been associated specifically with the entry of the Amorites into Mesopotamia, or with the movement of Amorites generally. Some of the place names of Mesopotamia share the names of Abraham's family – Haran, Nahor and Peleg, and others. The Amorites became, however, in the history of the Israelites' conquest of the Promised Land, merely a remnant of those who had ruled in the Babylonian region of Mesopotamia at the beginning of the second millennium BC, and who, ultimately, entered into a partnership with the Canaanites when forced to move west. Certainly by the time that the Israelites were spreading from the wilderness, the Amorites had been reduced to an annoyance in the hill country by previous Egyptian dominance of the land. According to the table of nations in the grand scheme of Genesis 10, the Amorites were descendants of Noah's grandson, Canaan.

Having refused the Israelites safe passage through his land, King Sihon of the Amorites fell victim to the Israelites east of the Dead Sea. 'Israel then sent messengers to King Sihon of the Amorites, king of Heshbon, and Israel said to him, "Let us pass through your land to our country."' But Sihon did not trust Israel to pass through his territory; so Sihon gathered all his people together, and encamped at Jahaz, and fought with Israel. Then the Lord, the God of Israel, gave Sihon and all his people into the hand of Israel, and they defeated them; so Israel occupied all the land of the Amorites, who inhabited that country. They occupied all the territory of the Amorites from the Arnon to the Jabbok and from the wilderness to the Jordan' (Judges 11.19–22).

(see *Babylonians, Habiru, Hurrians, Sumerians*)

Diagram
Map of the Fertile Crescent (5)

Ancestors of King David
Tree of the Royal Line of David

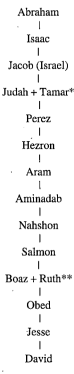

Abraham
|
Isaac
|
Jacob (Israel)
|
Judah + Tamar*
|
Perez
|
Hezron
|
Aram
|
Aminadab
|
Nahshon
|
Salmon
|
Boaz + Ruth**
|
Obed
|
Jesse
|
David

*Tamar was a Canaanitess and thereby the seed of a descendant of Noah's son Ham was joined to the line of David. Tamar was the widow of Judah's firstborn son Er, and mother of Perez by a devious ploy (Genesis 38).
**Ruth was a Moabitess and thereby the seed of a descendant of Lot was joined to the line of David (Ruth 4).
(see also *Writers of the Old Testament – Ruth* and Matthew 1)

Diagrams,
Descent of Abraham (1)
Family of Abraham (2)

Ancestors of King Saul

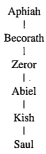

Aphiah
|
Becorath
|
Zeror
|
Abiel
|
Kish
|
Saul

'There was a man of Benjamin whose name was Kish' (1 Samuel 9.1 and 10).

Of Saul's children, Jonathan – the devoted friend of David – (1 Samuel 19 and 20) Abinadad and Malchishua died in battle against the Philistines; Ish-bosheth (Ish-baal) was declared king of the northern tribes, on his father's death, but was later murdered (2 Samuel 2.8–11 and 4.1–12); Michal, Saul's younger daughter, was given to David by Saul as wife and was subsequently given to another. After Saul's death, David demanded Michal's return and she was returned to him. Michal bore no children (1 Samuel 18.17–30; 25.42–44; 2 Samuel 3.13–15; 6.23).

Apostles

The original Greek word, apostle, means one who is commissioned to carry out a task. However, when the term is used in the Gospels, it is reserved for the Twelve, the disciples closest to Jesus. After the Ascension (Acts 1.6–11), the writers of the New Testament invariably refer to the Twelve as apostles. (The number twelve was preserved at the instigation of Peter, when a choice was made between Barsabbas and Matthias as the replacement for Judas Iscariot. 'And they cast lots for them, and the lot fell on Matthias; and he was added to the eleven apostles' (Acts 1.26).)

Paul refers to himself as an apostle, though he was not one of the Twelve, because he received his commission from Jesus. 'Paul, a servant of Jesus Christ, called to be an apostle set apart for the gospel of God, which he promised beforehand through his prophets in the holy scriptures' (Romans 1.1, 2). 'Paul, called to be an apostle of Christ Jesus' (1 Corinthians 1.1) see also (Acts 13.9; 9.1–31).

In the Early Church, and later, the term came to apply to all those who were sent out on missionary work as well as to those who had the authority to send missionaries.

(see also *Disciples of Jesus*)

Arameans

The Arameans appeared in the area of northern Syria towards the end of the second millennium BC, perhaps, about the time of the Exodus. They soon developed a fairly substantial kingdom based around Damascus. The Arameans feature significantly in the life of the people of the united Israel, and, later, after the division of the kingdom. King David subdued Damascus and, later, in the ninth century, Kings Omri and Ahab of Israel fought successfully against the Arameans. Later still, they entered a

17

coalition against the Assyrians. However, Assyria defeated the Arameans in 732 BC, ten years before sacking Samaria, the capital of the northern kingdom of Israel, and taking a great many of the Israelites into captivity.

The Arameans may have been a branch of the expanding Amorites associated with the general movement of Amorites from the Arabian Desert up through Mesopotamia, where they settled, some spreading into Syria and some into Canaan, all around the time of Abraham's movements from Ur to Haran and then into Canaan. The biblical ancestry of the Israelites is closely associated with the Arameans. Both Laban and his father, Bethuel, great nephew and nephew of Abraham respectively, are referred to as Arameans (Genesis 25.20). The retrospective reconstruction of the ancestry of and the brotherhood of the Semitic people is revealed in part of the grand table of the nations in Genesis 10.21.

Arkites

One of the descendant races of Canaan, the son of Ham and grandson of Noah.
(see *Canaanites*)

Diagram
Descent of Abraham (1)

Arvadites

The inhabitants of the Phoenician city of Arvad.
(see *Phoenicians*)

Ashdodites

The inhabitants of the Philistine city of Ashdod.
(see *Philistines*)

Asher, Tribe of

Asher was the eighth of Jacob's sons, the second by Zilpah, the servant of Jacob's wife Leah. 'Leah's maid Zilpah bore Jacob a second son. And Leah said, "Happy am I! For the women will call me happy"; so she named him Asher' (Genesis 30.12, 13). He was the ancestor of the tribe of Asher, which was allocated the highlands west of Galilee bordering the coastal state of the Phoenicians, and sandwiched between that state and the tribal land of Naphtali (Joshua 19.24–31).

Diagrams
Children of Israel (3)
Tribal Lands of Israel (8)

Assyrians

A people whose activities had a profound effect on the history of the Children of Israel. Assyria emerged, around 1300 BC, from the dominance of Mesopotamia (from the Greek words meaning 'between the rivers', in this case, the Tigris and the Euphrates) by the Hittite Empire. Assyria continued to be a force to be reckoned with even though its fortunes were mixed, until only a few decades before the destruction of its capital, Nineveh, in 612 BC.

Assyria's most formidable period, certainly from the perspective of the two kingdoms of Israel and Judah, arrived in *c*.745 BC with its new king, Tiglath-pileser III, who attacked both the Arameans and the northern part of the kingdom of Israel. 'In the days of King Pekah of Israel, King Tiglath-pileser of Assyria came and captured Ijon, Abel-beth-maacah, Janoath, Kedesh, Hazor, Gilead, and Galilee, all the land of Naphtali; and he carried the people captive to Assyria' (2 Kings 15.29). Tiglath-pileser's successor, Shalmaneser V, captured King Hoshea of Israel and imprisoned him (2 Kings 17.3, 4) but Samaria – the capital of the northern kingdom of Israel – ultimately fell to Sargon II in 722–721 BC. Tens of thousands of Israelites were subsequently deported to Nineveh. 'Then the king of Assyria invaded all the land and came to Samaria; for three years he besieged it. In the ninth year of Hoshea, the king of Assyria captured Samaria; he carried the Israelites away to Assyria' (2 Kings 17.5, 6a) Under Sennacherib, Assyria besieged Jerusalem during King Hezekiah's reign in Judah, but it did not fall to the Assyrians. After Assyria's final decline, Nineveh fell to a coalition of Babylonians, Medes and Scythians.

The retrospective reconstruction of the genealogy of and the brotherhood of the Semitic people is recorded in part of the grand table of the nations in Genesis 10.21. Asshur was reckoned to be the father of the Assyrians.

(see *Akkadians, Amorites, Babylonians, Elamites, Sumerians*)

Diagrams
Map of the Fertile Crescent (5)
Broad Parallel Histories (17–21)

Babylonians

A people vying first with the Hittites and others, then with the Assyrians, for supremacy in Mesopotamia (from the Greek words meaning 'between the rivers'; in this case, the Tigris and the Euphrates) from about 1830 BC after the fall of the Sumerian Empire at Ur, which had succumbed to the Amorites rising from the Arabian Desert. The Sumerians had already been made vulnerable by the attacks of the Elamites reigning down upon them from modern-day Iran. (During this period we must place the beginning of the wanderings of Abraham's family (Genesis 11.27–32).) Meanwhile, the Hurrians were infiltrating from the Caucasus mountains. The Amorites established the first Babylonian Empire, which lasted over two hundred years, finally giving way to the supremacy of the Old Hittite Empire for one hundred years. The kingdom of Mitanni, whose majority was, by now, the infiltrating Hurrians, dominated until the New Hittite Empire established itself between 1375 and 1200 BC. From about the time of the Exodus of the Israelites from Egypt in the thirteenth century BC, the Assyrians began to emerge as Mesopotamia's most significant presence and largely remained so with fluctuations in its fortunes until, in 612 BC, its capital at Nineveh was destroyed by a coalition of Babylonians, Medes and Scythians. (By that time, Assyria had dealt a deathly blow against the northern kingdom of Israel with the destruction of its capital, Samaria, and the deportation of tens of thousands of Israelites to Nineveh.)

The Babylonians emerged from the destruction of Nineveh in great strength and established themselves in the second (or new) Babylonian Empire when Assyria was all but annihilated. This Babylonian Empire was responsible for the capitulation of the southern kingdom of Judah with Nebuchadnezzar's destruction of Jerusalem and the deportation of many to Babylon. 'King Jehoiachin of Judah gave himself up to the king of Babylon, himself, his mother, his servants, his officers, and his palace officials. The king of Babylon took him prisoner in the eighth year of his reign. He carried off all the treasures of the house of the Lord, and the treasures of the king's house; he cut in pieces all the vessels of gold in the temple of the Lord, which King Solomon of Israel had made, all this as the Lord had foretold. He carried away all Jerusalem, all the officials, all the warriors, ten thousand captives, all the artisans and the smiths; no one remained, except the poorest people of the land' (2 Kings 24.12–14). Nebuchadnezzar's grandson, Belshazzar, was regent for his father, Nabonidus, when Cyrus the Great and the Persians took Babylon in 538 BC. 'In the first year of King Cyrus of Persia, in fulfilment of the word of the Lord spoken by Jeremiah, the Lord stirred up the spirit of King Cyrus of Persia so that he sent a herald throughout all his kingdom and also declared in a written edict: "Thus says King Cyrus of Persia: The Lord, the God of heaven, has given me all the kingdoms of the earth, and he has charged me to build a house at Jerusalem, which is in Judah. Whoever is among you of all his people, may the Lord his God be with him! Let him go up."' (2 Chronicles 36.22, 23).

(see *Akkadians, Amorites, Assyrians, Habiru, Hittites, Hurrians, Sumerians*)

Diagrams
Map of the Fertile Crescent (5)
Broad Parallel Histories (16–22)

Benjamin, Tribe of

Benjamin – Jacob's twelfth and last son – was born to Jacob's wife, Rachel. 'Then they journeyed from Bethel; and when they were still some distance from Ephrath, Rachel was in childbirth, and she had a difficult labour. When she was in her difficult labour, the midwife said to her, "Do not be afraid; for now you will have another son." As her soul was departing (for she died), she named him Ben-oni, but his father called him Benjamin' (Genesis 35.16–18). Benjamin was Jacob's favourite son, and ancestor of the tribe of Benjamin, which was allocated the land between Judah (the principal southern tribe) and Ephraim (one of the two Josephite tribes, and, ultimately, the principal northern tribe) (Joshua 18.11–28). At the division of Israel into the kingdoms of Israel and Judah, the tribe of Benjamin supported and sided with Judah. 'When Rehoboam came to Jerusalem, he assembled all the house of Judah and the tribe of Benjamin' (1 Kings 12.21a).

Diagrams
Children of Israel (3)
Tribal Lands of Israel (8)

Brothers of Jesus

Scholars and theologians have for centuries wrestled with the question of Jesus' 'brothers'. The 'brothers' are referred to from time to time in the New Testament. 'While he was still speaking to the crowds, his mother and his brothers were standing outside, wanting to speak to him' (Matthew 12.46). 'Is not this the carpenter's son? Is not his mother called Mary? And are not his brothers James and Joseph and Simon and Judas?' (Matthew 13.55). 'So his brothers said to him, "Leave here and go to Judea so that your disciples also may see the works you are doing; for no one who wants to be widely known acts in secret. If you do these things, show yourself to the world." (For not even his brothers believed in him.)' (John 7.3–5).

It is true that there are many occasions in the Bible when 'brother' is used in place of cousin, half-brother, step-brother, or some other relation entirely. And doubts arise as to whether these brothers are indeed uterine brothers when collating the accounts of the women at the cross from all four Gospels. If we identify 'Mary the mother of James and Joseph' (Matthew 27.56) with the mother of 'James and Joseph and Simon and Judas' (Matthew 13.55) [At the time the Gospels were written it may have been sufficient to identify the mother of these sons by citing the most well known of them. James (not one of the two of that name who numbered among Jesus' disciples) was probably, after the resurrection of Jesus, the leader of the Church in Jerusalem.] and with 'Mary the wife of Clopas' (John 19.25) we may conclude that this Mary was close to the mother of Jesus and, perhaps, part of an extended family. There is, then, nothing surprising about the James, Joseph, Simon and Judas (if all four were there) waiting in the company of Jesus' mother. Maybe Clopas was a brother of Joseph. None of the four named above was, incidentally, a disciple of Jesus before the crucifixion 'For not even his brothers believed in him' (John 7.5). This certainly is made clear by 'as well as his brothers' following a list of the eleven remaining disciples immediately after the Ascension narrative (Acts 1.12-14). There is also the possibility that in Mark 6: 3 the writer has simply confused the two Marys.

Also at the cross were 'the mother of the sons of Zebedee' (Matthew 27.56) 'Salome' (Mark 15.40) and Jesus' 'mother's sister' (John 19.25). But were these three women one and the same? They probably were.

If the four brothers were uterine brothers of Jesus would they not have seen it as their duty to take care of their mother after Jesus' crucifixion? Why should Jesus insult his brothers by placing his mother into the hands of one of his disciples? The above conjecture has appeal. Furthermore, if we can identify 'the disciple whom he [Jesus] loved' (John 19.26) as the disciple John and son of Zebedee and Salome, the placing of the care of his mother into the hands of a favourite young cousin seems perfectly reasonable.

For the most part, Protestant Christians have been content to accept James, Joseph, Simon, and Judas as Jesus' uterine brothers; Orthodox Christians have always favoured the belief that the four were sons of an earlier marriage of Joseph and, indeed, there was a strong non-canonical tradition that Joseph was an older man, and a widower; and Catholic Christians have, certainly in the past, favoured the belief that the four were cousins. In an endeavour to write down, as quickly as possible, the essential message of the gospel, this sort of biographical detail was omitted by the evangelists.

(see *Women at the Cross of Jesus and at the Tomb*)

Diagram
Brothers of Jesus (13)

Canaanites

According to the writers of Genesis, descendants of Canaan, the son of Ham and grandson of Noah. 'Canaan became the father of Sidon his firstborn, and Heth, and the Jebusites, the Amorites, the Girgashites, the Hivites, the Arkites, the Sinites, the Arvadites, the Zemarites, and the Hamathites. Afterwards the families of the

Carites

Canaanites spread abroad. And the territory of the Canaanites extended from Sidon, in the direction of Gerar, as far as Gaza, and in the direction of Sodom, Gomorrah, Admah, and Zeboiim, as far as Lasha' (Genesis 10.15–19).

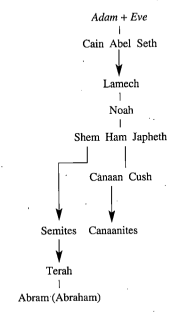

The Canaanites were the inhabitants of Canaan who, by the time of the Exodus and the expansion of the Hebrews from the wilderness, were a collection of many tribes, descended from the remnants of the numerous bands of settlers and invaders and who had aimed for or chanced upon the land over the centuries. They were unable to resist effectively the determined entry into the land by the Israelites. (However, the Israelites eventually settled alongside the populations they found in Canaan (Judges 3.1–6).) Originally, the Canaanites were a people who had begun to settle the land around 3000 BC and who were later joined by Amorites as they were pushed from Mesopotamia. Together, they were at their most formidable during the first half of the second millennium BC. In New Testament times, the name 'Canaanite' was often used as a substitute for 'Zealot'.
(see *Habiru, Hebrews and Zealots*)

Diagram
Map of Canaan (6)

Carites

Believed to have been Philistine mercenaries originally from Caria in the south west of Asia Minor (2 Kings 11.4).

22

Chaldeans

The inhabitants of Chaldea, an area of Babylonia, which probably encompassed Ur and the land south east of the coast of what is now the Persian Gulf. This was the land of Abram's (Abraham's) family. 'Now these are the descendants of Terah. Terah was the father of Abram, Nahor, and Haran; and Haran was the father of Lot. Haran died before his father Terah in the land of his birth, in Ur of the Chaldeans' (Genesis 11.27, 28). The name *Chaldea* is drawn from the Babylonian name for that area. However, to the writer of Jeremiah, for example, *Chaldea* and *Chaldeans* are synonymous with *Babylon* and *Babylonians*. 'Then after seventy years are completed, I will punish the king of Babylon and that nation, the land of the Chaldeans, for their iniquity, says the Lord, making the land an everlasting waste' (Jeremiah 25.12). 'I will repay Babylon and all the inhabitants of Chaldea before your very eyes for all the wrong that they have done in Zion, says the Lord' (Jeremiah 51.24).

Confusingly, in the king's court of Babylon, in the book of Daniel, *Chaldeans* seem to be wise men, soothsayers or astrologers. 'The king cried aloud to bring in the enchanters, the Chaldeans, and the diviners; and the king said to the wise men of Babylon' (Daniel 5.7). However, a little later we have 'Belshazzar, the Chaldean king, was killed' (Daniel 5.30).

(see *Amorites, Babylonians, Prophets – Daniel* and *Sumerians*)

Diagram
Map of the Fertile Crescent (5)

Characters of the Creation and Great Flood stories

Adam

The two creation stories are very different. In the one, God creates the world and sets mankind down into the heart of his creation. In the other, man is first created, and then the world filled around him. Both reveal different facets of the same story. Mankind is crafted to live in a specially created world already available for him. (This is, of course, creation by evolution.) At the same time, man is the first intention of the Creator, and so the world is made for him (Genesis 1, 2). Through disobedience to the will of God, Adam and Eve are cast out of the Garden of Eden to fend for themselves (Genesis 3).

Cain and Abel, sons of Adam and Eve

The point of the Cain and Abel parable (Genesis 4.1–7) is that evil is waiting to grasp the man who is disgruntled. It lurks at the door in the form of a desire to sin, the implication being that this desire was awakened by the disobedience of Adam and Eve. Cain seeks out Abel and murders him and is banished to a place east of Eden.

Seth

The third son of Adam and Eve is the ancestor of Noah and, therefore, the ancestor of a rescued humanity, the ancestor of both Semite and Canaanite.

Children of Israel

Noah

Eight generations after Seth, the earth is already populated but it is corrupt and it is time for a clean sweep. God instructs Noah to build an ark to withstand the forthcoming rains and flooding. He is to conserve pairs of all creatures within the ark and so allow life on earth to continue when the ark has come to rest again on dry land. Through his sons Noah is responsible for repopulating the earth.

Shem

The first son of Noah and the ancestor of Terah and, consequently, all Semites.

Ham

The second son of Noah and the father of Canaan, the ancestor of the Canaanites.

Diagram
Descent of Abraham (1)

Children of Israel

In the narrow sense, the Children of Israel are the children of Isaac's son, Jacob, whom God renamed, Israel. 'God appeared to Jacob again when he came from Paddan-aram, and he blessed him. God said to him, "Your name is Jacob; no longer shall you be called Jacob, but Israel shall be your name." So he was called Israel' (Genesis 35.9, 10).

In the wider sense, the Children of Israel are the nation of Israel in that after Joseph – Jacob's eleventh son – had established himself in Egypt, Jacob took the whole of his family there. 'When Israel set out on his journey with all that he had and came to Beer-sheba, he offered sacrifices to the God of his father Isaac. God spoke to Israel in visions of the night, and said, "Jacob, Jacob." And he said, "Here I am." Then he said, "I am God, the God of your father; do not be afraid to go down to Egypt, for I will make of you a great nation there. I myself will go down with you to Egypt, and I will also bring you up again; and Joseph's own hand shall close your eyes"' (Genesis 46.1–4). Jacob's last word to his twelve sons concludes with: 'All these are the twelve tribes of Israel, and this is what their father said to them when he blessed them, blessing each one of them with a suitable blessing' (Genesis 49.28).

In Egypt Israel became a sizeable nation and, after a time, the pharaoh of Egypt enslaved the Children of Israel: they were no longer tolerated sharing the life of the people of Egypt. Under Moses and Aaron, the Children of Israel fled the land of Egypt. (Exodus) After settling in the desert outside Egypt, they prepared to claim the 'Promised Land' the land promised to their forefather, Abraham. 'Abram passed through the land to Shechem, to the oak of Moreh. At that time the Canaanites were in the land. Then the Lord appeared to Abram, and said, "To your offspring I will give this land"' (Genesis 12.6, 7a). 'When Abram was ninety-nine years old, the Lord appeared to Abram, and said to him, "I am God Almighty; walk before me, and be blameless. And I will make a covenant between me and you, and will make you exceedingly numerous." Then Abram fell on his face; and God said to him, "As for me, this is my covenant with you: You shall be the ancestor of a multitude of nations. No longer shall your name be Abram, but your name shall be Abraham; for I have made you the ancestor of a multitude of nations"' (Genesis 17.1–5).

When the Children of Israel passed out of the desert region, they began their campaigns against the Canaanites and established themselves in the 'Promised Land' in the names of the twelve tribes. (Joshua)

The deacon, Stephen, gives a delightfully succinct history of Israel in Acts 7. (see *People of the Exodus, the Wilderness and the Entry into Canaan*)

Diagrams
Descent of Abraham (1)
Family of Abraham (2)
Children of Israel (3)
Tree of the Tribe of Levi (4)
Tribal Lands of Israel (8)
Broad Parallel Histories (16–22)

Chosen People

Throughout the Old Testament the writers constantly remind hearers and readers that the Children of Israel are God's *chosen*, a privilege so often taken for granted. As *chosen* people they have a special relationship with God and, consequently, a special responsibility to be faithful to him. The story of the Children of Israel is the story of God's revelation of himself through his prophets and through the unfolding of the history of the Children of Israel. They are *chosen* because God chose them to be the people to whom and through whom he manifested himself. 'O offspring of his servant Israel, children of Jacob, his chosen ones' (1 Chronicles 16.13). 'For the Lord has chosen Jacob for himself, Israel as his own possession' (Psalm 135.4). 'But you, Israel, my servant, Jacob, whom I have chosen, the offspring of Abraham, my friend; you whom I took from the ends of the earth, and called from its farthest corners, saying to you, "you are my servant, I have chosen you"' (Isaiah 41.8,9a). And in the Christian Era, it is within the context of the Chosen People that Jesus is revealed as Saviour of all mankind.

Christians

In the context of the New Testament, Christians, as now, are those who belong to the Christian Church; who believe in Jesus as the Christ, the Messiah; and who follow Jesus' example and teaching. The term is used only three times in the New Testament: Christians did not consistently use the term of themselves until about the second century. 'Then Barnabas went to Tarsus to look for Saul, and when he had found him, he brought him to Antioch. So it was that for an entire year they associated with the church and taught a great many people, and it was at Antioch that the disciples were first called "Christians"' (Acts 11.25, 26). 'Agrippa said to Paul, "Are you so quickly persuading me to become a Christian?"' (Acts 26.28). 'Yet if any of you suffers as a Christian, do not consider it a disgrace, but glorify God because you bear this name' (1 Peter 4.16).

Colossians

The inhabitants of the Phrygian city of Colossae. They were the addressees of a letter written by Paul, or in his name.
(see *Letter Writers of the New Testament – The Letter to the Colossians*)

Corinthians

The inhabitants of the city of Corinth, fifty miles west of Athens. They were the addressees of two letters by Paul.

(see *Letter Writers of the New Testament – The First and Second Letters to the Corinthians*)

Cushites

Cush, in the Old Testament, is the region to the south of Egypt – i.e. Ethiopia. It was under the domination of Egypt from the beginning of the second millennium BC until the Cushites pushed north and established an Ethiopian dynasty during the first half of the seventh century BC. This was annihilated by the Assyrians but not before King Tirhakah of Cush (or Ethiopia) had launched an attack on King Sennacherib of Assyria. 'When the king heard concerning King Tirhakah of Ethiopia, "See he has set out to fight against you"' (2 Kings 19.9).

The Cushites – apparently not the Ethiopian Cushites – were descendants of Cush, the son of Ham and grandson of Noah. According to the Noah saga in Genesis 10, Cush peopled the lands of southern Arabia. It is difficult, therefore, to identify the Cushites of Ethiopia with those of southern Arabia as the Red Sea separated the two countries and, furthermore, the Arabian Cushites, in the person of Nimrod, moved north into Mesopotamia. 'From that land he went into Assyria, and built Nineveh' (Genesis 10.11a).

Does 'Then all the officials sent Jehudi son of Nethaniah son of Shelemiah son of Cushi [i.e. 'the Cushite'] to say to Baruch' (Jeremiah 36.14) refer to an Arabian Cushite or, perhaps, to a descendant of an Ethiopian slave?

(see *Nubians*)

Diagram
Descent of Abraham (1)

Dan, Tribe of

Dan was the fifth son of Jacob and the first of the two born to Rachel's servant, Bilhah. 'And Bilhah conceived and bore Jacob a son. Then Rachel said, "God has judged me and has also heard my voice and given me a son"; therefore she named him Dan' (Genesis 30.5, 6). He was the ancestor of the tribe of Dan, which was first allocated land south of the land of Ephraim between the land of Benjamin and the coastal land of the Philistines. (Joshua 19.40–48) After failing to secure this territory, the Danites moved north to the region beyond the land of the tribe of Naphtali. (Judges 18) The two tribes had camped together, along with the tribe of Asher, in the wilderness at Sinai. (Numbers 2.25–31) There was a natural affinity between the two tribes of Dan and Naphtali descending as they did from the two sons of Jacob by Bilhah.

Diagrams
Children of Israel (3)
Tribal Lands of Israel (8)

Deacons, seven

Even though the Greek word *diakonos* is not employed at all in the Acts of the Apostles, the seven appointed and ordained to serve at table are generally referred to as the seven deacons. They were 'seven men of good standing, full of the Spirit and of wisdom' (Acts 6.3) and were appointed to assist the apostles by relieving them of some of their duties. 'They [the community of the disciples at Jerusalem, i.e. the Christian community] had these men stand before the apostles, who prayed and laid their hands on them' (Acts 6.6).

Nothing is known of Prochorus, Nicanor, Timon, and Parmenas. Nicholaus was a proselyte of Antioch, a Greek convert to Judaism. Of Stephen and Philip we know a little more. 'Stephen, full of grace and power, did great wonders and signs among the people' (Acts 6.8). When he was hauled before the council of the Jews (the Sanhedrin) on a charge of blasphemy, he answered the charge with great eloquence. 'And Stephen replied: . . .' (Acts 7.2-53) 'Then they dragged him out of the city and began to stone him' (Acts 7.58–60). Stephen was the Church's first martyr. Philip was referred to as 'the evangelist' and had settled in Caesarea. '. . . and we went into the house of Philip the evangelist, one of the seven, and stayed with him. He had four unmarried daughters who had the gift of prophecy' (Acts 21.8, 9). The stories of Philip's preaching in Samaria and of the Ethiopian eunuch's desire for baptism can be found in Acts 8.

Diaspora

The name given to the dispersion of the Israelites from Palestine. The Israelites were transported to Nineveh in the eighth century BC and to Babylon in the sixth century BC, and settlements developed there and farther east. There were also settlements in Egypt and, eventually, throughout the Mediterranean. These communities kept in touch with their homeland through the payment of Temple tax and by travelling to Jerusalem at festival time. 'Now there were devout Jews from every nation under heaven living in Jerusalem' (Acts 2.5). There is a reference to the Diaspora in John 7.35, and James addresses his letter 'To the twelve tribes in the Dispersion'.

Disciples of Jesus

There is no doubt that the disciples of Jesus were numerous. But within the crowds who clamoured to hear him preach there would have been occasional followers and those who could not make up their minds about him. Inevitably, there would have been those who were not necessarily interested in anything Jesus had to say but simply in attendance to keep an eye and an ear on him and his associates, as his popularity grew. We know that the crowds would often number in their thousands: 'For there were about five thousand men' (Luke 9.14); 'Those who had eaten were four thousand men, besides women and children' (Matthew 16.38).

Of all his disciples – i.e. those under his discipline – we know little. Characters appear during the narratives of the Gospels in order that the evangelist might draw attention to a particular teaching of Jesus. Many of these characters were probably disciples (or would-be disciples) of Jesus, or would become disciples. We know from the Acts of the Apostles, though not from the Gospels, that, for example, Joseph Barsabbas and Matthias accompanied the Twelve 'from the baptism of John until the day he [Jesus] was taken up' (Acts 1.22a). We know also that from hundreds

27

Disciples of Jesus

of faithful and dedicated followers Jesus selected seventy missionaries to preach and heal on the occasion recorded in Luke 10. And before that, Jesus had sent the Twelve on a similar mission giving them in his instructions an intensive lesson in discipleship: 'and he sent them out to proclaim the kingdom of God and to heal' (Luke 9.2) and 'These twelve Jesus sent out with the following instruction' (Matthew 10.5–25).

The Twelve were Jesus' close associates and those who would form the kernel of the Early Church. Their questions, their mistakes and their foolishness are recorded in the Gospels so that Jesus' responses can instruct the readers and hearers of the Gospels. In the Gospel of John, we hear that Jesus' first disciples were drawn from those of John the Baptist. Indeed, it was John who had pointed out Jesus to them as 'the Lamb of God' (John 1.36b) The gathering of the first disciples recorded in the Gospel of Luke reveals that before the sons of Zebedee were called, Simon Peter was already an associate of Jesus; and the accounts in the Gospels of Matthew and Mark record the occasion from a slightly different point of view. Of course, it is likely that the sons of Zebedee were first cousins of Jesus and, therefore, would have already known Jesus well enough. The Gospels, however, do not provide us with full details of the calling of all twelve; indeed, some of the individuals are hardly mentioned.

That Jesus selected an 'inner circle' of Simon Peter and the two sons of Zebedee is clear from the Gospels; as it is clear that Simon Peter was singled out by Jesus at the beginning of his gathering of the disciples, as the senior man for the future, the rock upon which the Early Church would stand. '"You are Simon son of John. You are to be called Cephas" (which is translated Peter)' (John 1.42b). [*Kepha* is Aramaic for rock and *Petra* is the Greek translation.] .

Diagram
Disciples of Jesus (14)

Judas Iscariot

The son of Simon Iscariot (John 6.71), a Judean, and treasurer – though not necessarily an honest one – to Jesus and the other close disciples (John 12.6). Iscariot (ish Kariot) means man of Kerioth, presumably, the region in south Palestine whence the family originally came. It is likely that this Judas was of the party of Zealots who were anxious to see a Messiah at the head of a powerful and irresistible uprising against the Romans. Judas betrayed Jesus either because he had become disillusioned, or because he genuinely, though mistakenly, thought he could precipitate the coming and the triumph of the kingdom of God. Perhaps the former is the more likely.

Simon the Zealot

This Simon is named 'Simon the Canaanite' in the Gospels of Matthew and Mark, but 'Simon the Zealot' in the Gospel of Luke (Matthew 10.2–4; Mark 3.16–19; Luke 6.15). There need be no confusion because, here, Canaanite is simply the Aramaic equivalent of Zealot. Simon was, initially anyway, of the faction favouring armed insurrection.

Judas (not Iscariot)

This Judas was the son of James (Luke 6.16) and probably identical with the Thaddaeus (or Lebbaeus in some sources) of Matthew 10.3 and Mark 3.18. 'Lord, how is it that you will reveal yourself to us, and not to the world?' Judas asks in John 14.22.

28

James II

James, son of Alphaeus and, therefore, probably the brother of Matthew, features in the same position in each of the lists of the Twelve – Matthew 10.2–4; Mark 3.16–19; Luke 6.14–16; Acts 1.13. This James is not likely to have been the brother of Joses and son of Mary as some have asserted. Those brothers are more likely to have been two of the four – James (we shall refer to him as James III), Joseph (Joses), Simon, and Judas – mentioned in Matthew 13.55.

(see *Brothers of Jesus*)

Matthew

Levi seems to have been renamed, Matthew, by Jesus. Matthew was the son of Alphaeus according to Mark 2.14 and, therefore, brother of James II, unless there were two fathers of the name Alphaeus. Matthew was a tax-gatherer for the Romans and, as such, would have been classed as a sinner by the Scribes and the Pharisees.

It is unlikely that Matthew was the author of the Gospel, but he might have been the source of a body of recollections used by the author.

Thomas

Thomas is, of course, a perfectly good Greek name. Misleadingly, in Aramaic it suggests another word meaning *twin* and for this reason Thomas was nicknamed *The Twin* despite the probability that he was no such thing! The writer of John's Gospel, by learnedly translating the nickname into Greek (Didymus), the language of the Gospel, encourages the reader to believe that Thomas was in fact a twin.

Thomas's doubt about the first resurrection appearance to the ten disciples enables the evangelist to record Jesus' words: 'Have you believed because you have seen me? Blessed are those who have not seen and yet have come to believe' (John 20.29) when Thomas is present on the occasion of the second appearance in the house.

In Matthew, Mark, and Luke, Thomas is listed as a disciple but does not feature in any narrative.

Nathanael Bartholomew

Bartholomew, or, rather, the son of Tolmai, appears in the lists of the Twelve given in Matthew 10.2–4; Mark 3.16–19; and Luke 6.14–16. He seems to be closely associated with and a friend of Philip who, in John 1.45–51, introduced Nathanael to Jesus. As Bartholomew is simply a family name, it is likely that Nathanael and Bartholomew were one and the same.

Philip

We are told of Philip's recruitment in John 1.43–44. Philip, a Greek who lived in Bethsaida, and, presumably, a friend of Nathanael, was responsible for introducing the latter to Jesus. Jesus' miracle of the feeding of the five thousand was his response to Philip's statement, 'Six months' wages would not buy enough bread for each of them to get a little' (John 6.7) which, in turn, was Philip's answer to Jesus' 'Where are we to buy bread for these people to eat?' (John 6.5).

Andrew

A partner in the Bethsaida fishing business, the brother of Simon Peter, and a follower of John the Baptist. Andrew, and another, stayed with Jesus after John the Baptist had pointed them to Jesus as 'the Lamb of God' (John 1.35–40). Andrew

Disciples of Jesus

introduced his brother to Jesus soon afterwards (John 1.41, 42). Andrew lived with Peter, along with Peter's wife and mother-in-law (Mark 1.29, 30). It was Andrew who, in John's account of the feeding of the five thousand, identified a source of food, albeit, rather doubtfully: 'There is a boy here who has five barley loaves and two fish. But what are they among so many people?' (John 6.8, 9).

Peter

Peter (i.e. the rock) – so Jesus surnamed Simon Bar-Jonah (i.e. Simon, son of John) – was of the 'inner circle' of the Twelve along with James and John, the sons of Zebedee. (Later, Peter was accustomed to taking his wife on his missionary journeys (1 Corinthians 9.5).) The 'inner circle' was privileged to accompany Jesus on special occasions: 'Jesus took with him Peter and John and James, and went up on the mountain to pray' (Luke 9.28).

Peter was a partner in the Bethsaida fishing business with his brother and the sons of Zebedee, and lived with his wife, mother-in-law, and brother, Andrew, in Capernaum. (Mark 1.29, 30) Jesus named him 'the rock' in John 1.44 as a challenge, something to live up to, and so justify Jesus' expectations of him. It was not an easy apprenticeship, soaring to the heights of joy at the beginning of Jesus' ministry: '"But who do you say that I am?" . . . Peter answered, "The Messiah of God"' (Luke 9.20), and plumbing the depths of fear and despair towards the end: 'Now Simon Peter was standing and warming himself. They asked him, "You are not also of his disciples, are you?" He denied it and said, "I am not"' (John 18.25).

The first part of the Acts of the Apostles reveals the importance of Peter in the Early Church in Jerusalem. After the death of James I, Peter was imprisoned but he escaped and 'Then he left and went to another place' (Acts 12.17b). James III 'the Less' succeeded him as leader in Jerusalem. (see *Brothers of Jesus*)

There is a very ancient tradition that Mark's Gospel draws substantially from Peter's preaching in Rome. It may be that this Mark and the John Mark of Acts 12.12 are one and the same and accompanied Peter on his missionary journeys after he was forced to leave Jerusalem. Peter was probably martyred in Rome about AD 64.

James I

James, the son of Zebedee and Salome, was one of the 'inner circle' of the Twelve along with his brother and Peter. He is referred to as James 'the Great' to distinguish him from the other disciple James (James II above) and from James 'the Less' who was later prominent in Jerusalem. (see *Brothers of Jesus*)

James I was 'killed with the sword' (Acts 12.2) at the instigation of Herod Agrippa I, about ten years after the crucifixion and resurrection.

John

The brother of James I above: the two brothers were nicknamed 'Boanerges' or 'Sons of Thunder' by Jesus, and both were of the 'inner circle' of disciples (Mark 3.17; Luke 9.51–55; Mark 9.2). Both brothers suffered the embarrassment of their mother's request of Jesus to allow them to sit on the left and right of Jesus in his kingdom (Matthew 20.20–28).

John is almost universally identified with 'the beloved disciple' (or, in the translation used in this book 'the disciple whom Jesus loved') and there is a strong case for this identification. Although it is unlikely that John himself wrote any of the books in the New Testament whose authors claimed that name, it is not unreasonable to suggest that the author of the Gospel of John relied upon the disciple's recollections in some form or another. As, perhaps, a reflection of and respect for the disciple's own modesty, the author refrains from identifying 'the beloved disciple' at both the last supper (John 13.25) and also at the foot of the cross (John 19.26, 27). However, that Jesus should place his mother into the care of a favourite cousin who had experienced the most profound moments of his ministry is hardly surprising.

(see *Friends, Relatives and Acquaintances of Jesus* and *Women at the Cross*)

Disciples of John the Baptist

John's disciples were numbered in 'crowds' (Luke 3.7, 10; Matthew 3.5, 6). He was clearly a popular preacher and baptized those who came to him confessing their sins. He left his followers in no doubt that he was merely the forerunner of the Messiah: 'but one who is more powerful than I is coming; I am not worthy to untie the thong of his sandals. He will baptize you with the Holy Spirit and fire' (Luke 3.16). In answer to the priests and Levites, he said, 'I am the voice of one crying out in the wilderness, "make straight the way of the Lord"' (John 1.23).

Some of Jesus' disciples had been disciples of or, at least, followers of John. Certainly Andrew was one and, indeed, Jesus himself numbered among the crowd. 'The next day John again was standing with two of his disciples, and as he watched Jesus walk by, he exclaimed, "Look, here is the Lamb of God!" . . . One of the two who heard John speak and followed him [Jesus] was Andrew, Simon Peter's brother' (John 1.35, 36, 40).

Had John and Jesus been members of the sect of the Essenes whose library was found in the caves at Qumran beside the Dead Sea? Some have made this speculation but the New Testament is silent on the subject and, in fact, no mention of the sect is made.

(see *Essenes*)

Edomites

The descendants of Esau. 'These are the descendants of Esau (that is, Edom)' (Genesis 36.1). Esau and Jacob were the sons of Isaac (Abraham's son) and Rebekah. 'When the boys grew up, Esau was a skilful hunter, a man of the field, while Jacob was a quiet man, living in tents' (Genesis 25.27). The story-teller here indicates the contrast in the nature of the lives of their descendants, which certainly gives an accurate picture of the Edomites and of the Israelites up to the time that the latter finally settled in the land of Canaan.

The story of the difficulties of the relationship between the brothers is told in chapters 25–33 of Genesis. '. . . and he (Esau) moved to a land some distance from his brother Jacob' (Genesis 36.6). 'So Esau settled in the hill country of Seir; Esau is Edom' (Genesis 36.8).

By the time that the Israelites were moving out of the wilderness following their Exodus from Egypt, Edom was a long-established kingdom south of the Dead Sea. To facilitate their convenient passage to the land of Canaan, Israel sought permission from the king to pass through the land of Edom. 'Thus says your brother Israel: You know all the adversity that has befallen us: . . . and when we cried to the Lord, he heard our voice, and sent an angel and brought us out of Egypt; and here we are in Kadesh, a town on the edge of your territory. Now let us pass through your land' (Numbers 20.14–17). The king of Edom denied Israel's request. 'Thus Edom refused to give Israel passage through their territory; so Israel turned away from them' (Numbers 20.27).

By the time of the David, Edom had been overcome (2 Samuel 8.11, 12) and, subsequently, in Solomon's day, the land of Edom was effectively within the control of Israel.

Diagrams
Family of Abraham (2)
Map of Canaan (6)

Egyptians

In about 5500 BC the Sahara Desert was pushing ever eastwards, carrying the seasonal settlements of semi-nomads with it on its leading edge. These people buried their dead and, more significantly, embalmed and mummified their dead. Eventually, they arrived in the Nile Valley, pushed there by the unrelenting desert, where other settlers must have preceded them. From these beginnings grew the great Egyptian civilization, its long and complex history making it a fascinating subject for closer study.

The early dynasties of Egypt lasted for about four hundred years from the end of the fourth millennium BC, and the period usually known as the Old Kingdom – the heyday of the finest pyramids – flourished until about the end of the third millennium BC. The regions of the Nile Valley and the Nile Delta became disunited for a short period until, once again, union was re-established and gave rise to the Middle Kingdom. About 250 years into the second millennium – perhaps about the time of Abraham – Egypt began to disintegrate under the influence of invaders and the incursions of the Hyksos. It was during this period that Jacob and his sons began to settle in Egypt. Gradually, Egypt again regained control of its territory following the rise to power of Ahmose (1570–1550 BC) and the influence of the New Kingdom ultimately reached as far as the river Euphrates. For about one hundred and fifty years from, say, 1550 BC, the Hebrews were less well tolerated in Egypt and fell into disfavour and were enslaved. 'Now a new king arose over Egypt, who did not know Joseph. He said to his people, "Look, the Israelite people are more numerous and more powerful than we. Come, let us deal shrewdly with them, or they will increase and, in the event of war, join our enemies and fight against us and escape from the land"' (Exodus 1.8–10). This culminated in the Exodus at the end of the reign of Seti I or at the beginning of the reign of Rameses II. Some would argue that Seti I was the pharaoh 'who did not know Joseph', but it is likely that the period of disfavour was rather longer. It is, of course, by no means certain that the Exodus took place during the reigns of either Seti I or Rameses II.

During the time of the Judges in Israel, Egypt's influence outside its borders lessened, and the region of the Nile Delta gave way to invaders from Libya as King David was establishing his kingdom in Israel. After the division of the kingdom of Israel, one of the Libyan kings – Shishak – invaded Rehoboam's southern kingdom of Judah and 'he took away the treasures of the house of the Lord and the treasures of the king's house; he took everything' (2 Chronicles 12.9). However, Egypt had already begun a final decline from which there was only temporary relief during the succeeding centuries. There were defeats and triumphs against Assyria, Judah and Babylon, but Egypt was dealt a deadly blow by Babylon at Carchemish in 605 BC.

Successively, Egypt was part of the Persian, Greek, Ptolemaic and Roman Empires. Under the Ptolemys, it was extremely prosperous; and it was renowned, in Roman times, as the wealthiest of the Roman provinces.

Diagram
Broad Parallel Histories (16–22)

Elamites

The Elamites entered the area behind southern Mesopotamia from the east, and settled there pushing into Mesopotamia in waves around 1950 BC. During these incursions Ur fell, and Sumeria became vulnerable to the determined advances of the Amorites rising up from the Arabian Desert into Canaan and Mesopotamia from the south. It was from the minor city-state of Anshan in Elam, by now in the Median Empire, that Cyrus the Great grew to prominence. He rebelled against the king of the Medes, succeeded him and, in a short time, had styled himself King of the Persians. In that wide-ranging table of the nations contained in Genesis 10.21, we find that the writers or compilers of Genesis saw the Elamites as a part of the world's brotherhood, as they had descended from Shem, a son of Noah.

Diagram
Map of the Fertile Crescent (5)

Ephraim, Tribe of

Ephraim was the second of the two sons of Joseph, the eleventh son of Jacob. Both sons were adopted by Jacob and became tribal ancestors along with their uncles. 'And Jacob said to Joseph, "God Almighty appeared to me at Luz in the land of Canaan, and blessed me, and said to me, 'I am going to make you fruitful and increase your numbers; I will make you a company of peoples, and will give this land to your offspring after you for a perpetual holding.' Therefore your two sons, who were born to you in the land of Egypt before I came to you in Egypt, are now mine; Ephraim and Manasseh shall be mine, just as Reuben and Simeon are"' (Genesis 48.3–5).The Josephite tribe of Ephraim was allocated land in the central part of Palestine below that of Manasseh and west of the river Jordan. (Joshua 16) Ephraim became synonymous with the kingdom of Israel after the division of the kingdoms.

Diagrams
Children of Israel (3)
Tribal Lands of Israel (8)

Epicureans and Stoics

Epicureanism and Stoicism were ancient Greek schools of Philosophy. Philosophers of these schools debated with Paul during his visit to Athens – 'So he argued in the synagogue with the Jews and the devout persons, and also in the market-place every day with those who happened to be there. Also some Epicurean and Stoic philosophers debated with him' (Acts 17.17, 18). In short, Epicureanism was the enjoyment of pleasure in the sense of happiness rather than sensual pleasure. It was a rather negative philosophy at this time and perhaps provided a helpful vacuum for the spread of the Christian gospel. Though the theology of Stoicism was pantheism, its moral philosophy was highly developed and, perhaps, not an unsympathetic ground in which to sow the seeds of Christianity.

Paul quotes the Stoic poet, Aratus, as he proclaims the gospel before the Areopagus: 'For we too are his offspring.' Paul continues 'Since we are God's offspring, we ought not to think that the deity is . . . formed by the art and imagination of mortals' (Acts 17.28, 29).

We do not know how many in Paul's Athenian audience were Epicureans or Stoics; and we do not know if Epicureans and Stoics numbered among those who were converted. '. . . some of them . . . became believers, including Dionysius the Areopagite and a woman named Damaris, and others with them' (Acts 17.34).

Essenes

According to the historian Pliny the Elder, the Essenes lived a communal life in the wilderness of Judea, beside the north-western tip of the Dead Sea. In 1947, what is likely to have been the library of the Essene community was discovered in eleven caves at Qumran. Translations of these 'Dead Sea Scrolls' as they came to be called, reveal that this community was a Jewish sect of monastic persuasion whose daily life comprised, for the most part, study and prayer.

There is no mention of the Essenes in the Bible – they probably existed from the second century BC to the second century AD – but they were clearly a part of the Jewish life of the time, even though they chose to withdraw to the ascetic life. Was there a connection between the Essene community and John the Baptist's appearance 'in the wilderness of Judea'? (Matthew 3.1) It is unlikely that his preaching would have seemed alien to the Essenes: perhaps he had spent time within their community. Did Jesus himself retire hereabouts to consider his ministry? 'And the Spirit immediately drove him out into the wilderness. He was in the wilderness for forty days' (Mark 1.12, 13).

Diagram
Map of the Holy Land (9)

Evangelists

Generally speaking, *evangelists* are preachers of the Christian gospel; when the word is used with a capital letter, it refers to the writers of the four Gospels of the New Testament. Who were these writers?

Although there is much common ground among Bible scholars about the likely dates of the four Gospels, agreement is by no means universal; and there are differences of opinion as to the sources drawn upon by the writers, and the extent to which one writer relied upon the work of another.

There can be no doubt, however, that the four Gospels – burning with the faith and the enthusiasm of the writers as they do – provide the foundation blocks, together with the other writings of the New Testament and the tradition of the Church, for the propagation and promulgation of the Christian faith. But enquiry into something of the generation of the Gospels is of benefit to our understanding. What the Gospels are not – and this is, perhaps, the cause of some frustration – are precise and meticulously documented biographies of Jesus, his family, friends and disciples. We have to glean what we can but our conclusions are, inevitably, conjectural. The aim of the writers of the Gospels was to collect, collate and interpret as best they could, the extraordinary experiences of those who were closest to Jesus throughout his ministry, death and resurrection.

Matthew

Matthew's Gospel was written in about AD 85, in Greek, by someone – his quotations from the Old Testament are numerous – who held largely Jewish-Christian views. The Gospel reveals a learning that suggests the author was not the tax-collecting Matthew, and, therefore, identification with the apostle of that name is not feasible. However, the writer may well have drawn from a written source, possibly in Aramaic, of the recollections and personal experience of the apostle Matthew. The writer of the Gospel seems to have used most of Mark's Gospel, and to have had access to another source of material unique to his Gospel. Furthermore, he seems to have shared a common source with the writer of Luke's Gospel – often named 'Q'.

Matthew's Gospel sees in Jesus the fulfilment of Israel's longing for the Messiah, and sets out a rule of life by which the work of the kingdom, proclaimed by Jesus himself, is to be carried out.'An account of the genealogy of Jesus the Messiah, the son of David, the son of Abraham' (Matthew 1.1).'And Jesus came and said to them, 'All authority in heaven and on earth has been given to me. Go therefore and make disciples of all nations, baptizing them in the name of the Father and of the Son and of the Holy Spirit, and teaching them to obey everything that I have commanded you. And remember, I am with you always, to the end of the age' (Matthew 28.18–20).

Mark

Mark's Gospel was written in Rome in about AD 65, probably by John Mark (Acts 12.2; Colossians 4.10), sometime companion of Paul but also companion of Peter in Rome. Peter's preaching in Rome and his eye witness testimony to the life, death and resurrection of Jesus may not be the only source of Mark's Gospel, however. The Gospel was written in colloquial Greek.

Mark's aim is to reveal and stress the *authority* of Jesus, an authority emanating from none other than God himself. So Mark, in his Gospel, answers the questions posed by the chief priests, scribes and elders when they ask Jesus: 'By what authority are you doing these things? Who gave you this authority to do them?' (Mark 11.28).

Luke

Both the Gospel of Luke and its sequel, the Acts of the Apostles, were written by one hand, and it is reasonable to accept the tradition that they were written by the physician Luke, who accompanied Paul on some of his journeys (Colossians 4.14). He was a Greek Gentile from Antioch and wrote the books in the AD 70s. His polished and literary Gospel is addressed to a non-Jewish world, perhaps also to the well-heeled. He uses Mark's Gospel, but not all of it, and the other source shared by Matthew, usually named 'Q'; in addition he has sources of his own, one of which may well have been Jesus' mother, Mary.

Luke's message is that God has, in the birth, death and resurrection of Jesus, faithfully fulfilled the promises made to Israel by opening his arms to the whole of mankind, to Gentiles and to those from all strata of society.'Then he said to them, 'These are my words that I have spoken to you while I was still with you – that everything written about me in the law of Moses, the prophets, and the psalms must be fulfilled' (Luke 24.44).

John

The John of the Fourth Gospel is not likely to have been the son of Zebedee, the cousin of Jesus, and apostle. The Gospel was written in about AD 90 – there is a strong tradition that the disciple John died not many years after his brother James was put to death by Herod Agrippa – and was aimed at the community that had begun in the small house-churches in Palestine. It draws from a number of sources unknown to the writers of the other Gospels, though the writer was possibly aware of at least the Gospels of Mark and Luke. Opinion is divided on whether or not the writer of the Gospel was the author of any of the three epistles of John. Some see a common hand – that of John the Elder – in all four works; others see the work of a pupil, in the second and third epistles. Is it, therefore, likely that the Gospels and all three letters at least arise out of the same school – that of the disciple John and his followers? Perhaps it is.

Does the fascinating fact that John the disciple is not mentioned at all in John's Gospel, suggest that he might well be the anonymous disciple referred to many times, from the companion of Andrew in John 1.35–41 (John was the son of the partner of Andrew and Peter) to the numerous references to the disciple 'whom Jesus loved'? Of course, Matthew is not mentioned in the Gospel either, but he hardly fits into this hypothesis. (Incidentally, John's Gospel does, of course, acknowledge that there were indeed twelve disciples (John 6.70).) That John was Jesus' first cousin, and one of the three disciples closest to Jesus, makes his presence beside the cross with Mary, the mother of Jesus, probable. It is difficult not to be persuaded that the disciple 'whom Jesus loved' and John the apostle are one and the same. If this is the case, is it not likely that John the apostle was the source of the eye-witness material used by the writer of the Gospel? Jesus' mother was the only other witness to the private and personal instructions: 'Woman, here is your son.' and 'Here is your mother.'(John 19.26, 27). But there are many propositions put forward by scholars.

The theology of the opening of the Gospel reveals the vast scale of the work: that alone sets it apart from the first three Gospels. 'In the beginning was the Word, and the Word was with God, and the Word was God. He was in the beginning with God. And the Word became flesh and lived among us, and we have seen his glory, the glory as of a father's only son, full of grace and truth' (John 1.1,2, 14).
(see *Letter Writers of the New Testament*)

Diagrams
Brothers of Jesus (13)
Evangelists and their sources (15)

Family of Adam and the Patriarchs

The events of the first part of Genesis take place at the creation of the world; even so, the writers are at pains to provide detail of the descent of mankind from Adam and Eve so that the emergence and history of Israel can be shown in a fairly seamless and uninterrupted narrative. Most of the material was not written down at all until after the division of Israel, following Solomon's death in 922 BC, and certainly not combined in anything like its present form until after the return from the Captivity, following the fall of Babylon in 539 BC.

The stories, customs, and traditions were preserved in the memory, and transmitted orally with great care and attention. The sweeping sagas of the creation (there are two very different creation stories both of which make powerful points about the intention of the Creator) (Genesis 1.26–2.25), the fall of mankind (Genesis 3), and saga of Noah (Genesis 6–9); are all epic stories that paint a back-drop for the events that follow – primarily the call of Abraham (Genesis 12), the promise to Abraham (Genesis 15), and the history of his descendants, in particular, his son Isaac (Genesis 21), whose son, Jacob, is renamed, Israel, by God himself (Genesis 32.28). The call of Moses (Exodus 3), the Exodus from Egypt (Exodus 12, 13, 14), and the conquest and settling of Canaan (Joshua and Judges), bring the history of God's Chosen People to the period of the Judges (Judges), the monarchy of Saul, David, Solomon, and the division of the kingdom (1 and 2 Samuel; 1 and 2 Kings; 1 and 2 Chronicles). (see *Patriarchs* and *Writers of the Old Testament*)

Diagrams
Descent of Abraham (1)
Family of Abraham (2)
Children of Israel (3)

Family of Jesus

Jesus

Jesus was born in Bethlehem in the reign of Herod the Great, 37– 4 BC. (Matthew 2.1) His year of birth was clearly no later than 4 BC but there is no clear consensus among scholars as to the precise date: some favour 12 BC when Halley's Comet made its periodic appearance. The death and Resurrection of Jesus occurred while Pontius Pilate was governor or procurator, between AD 27 and 36. (John 23.1) We know nothing of Jesus' childhood after his visit to the temple at the age of twelve, after which, we are told, 'Jesus increased in wisdom and in years, and in divine and human favour' (Luke 2.52). The next we hear of him is his baptism in the river Jordan; his temptation in the wilderness; and the beginning of his ministry, which may have lasted only three years.

Jesus was a carpenter as his guardian, Joseph, had been. (Mark 6.1–6) This information is given to us almost obliquely. But, was he a successful one? Was the time he spent in the wilderness before beginning his ministry, spent, say, testing his vocation with the Essenes? We do not know these things. They were of no importance in the minds of the Gospel writers, who had no intention of writing detailed biographical accounts of Jesus' life. Jesus' ministry, the revelation of his messiahship and his divinity, his death and Resurrection, were the important ingredients in the Gospels.

Through his life and example, his trial, death and Resurrection, Jesus shows us much more of God the Father, and throughout his ministry, Jesus is schooling his disciples for what must follow. He tests them. He teaches them by example, by preaching, by argument, through parables spoken and acted, and, sparingly, through miracles. His teaching was revolutionary – even some of the parables, whose stories were sometimes well known, were delivered in a fresh way, and often with an unconventional twist. (He taught by parable for those who had ears to hear, and by miracle for those who had eyes to see. For his teaching was presented on two levels – the actual story of the parable and the single and simple point the parable was making; the fact of the miracle and the significance of the miracle. And the evangelists are, more often than not, at pains to emphasize these two points and reveal them

37

by the careful placing of them within the narrative of the Gospel.) The Jewish authorities were determined to be rid of him. After all, he caused too much upheaval and, anyway, he could not be the Messiah because they had never been led to believe that the Messiah would be anything like Jesus of Nazareth! Their only hope was to charge him with an offence that would entitle them to place him before the Roman governor. They did so and the trial, crucifixion, death and Resurrection are recorded in all four Gospels.

When messengers came from John the Baptist to ask Jesus 'are you the one who is to come [i.e. the Messiah] or are we to look for another?' he replied: 'Go and tell John what you have seen and heard: the blind receive their sight, the lame walk, the lepers are cleansed, the deaf hear' (Luke 7.20,22). The message is clear and contained in Isaiah's Messianic passage – Isaiah 35.5, 6. Simon Peter points to the nub of it and reveals the divine nature of the Messiah when asked: '"But who do you say that I am?" Simon Peter answered, "You are the Messiah, the Son of the living God"' (Matthew 16.15, 16).

Joseph
The guardian of Jesus.
(see *Friends, Relations and Acquaintances of Jesus*)

Mary
The mother of Jesus.
(see *Brothers of Jesus, Essenes, Disciples, Friends, Relations and Acquaintances of Jesus, Prophets – Isaiah*)

Diagram
Brothers of Jesus (12)

Family of John the Baptist

Of the writers of the canonical Gospels only Luke gives us something of John the Baptist's family: in fact, he provides us with a good deal of information about the birth of John and of the characters of his father, Zechariah, and his mother, Elizabeth. Furthermore, he closely associates the family of Jesus with the family of John the Baptist.

The first chapter of the Gospel of Luke is set aside for the story of the circumstances of the birth of John, which is wrapped around the Annunciation to Mary (Luke 1.26–38) and the Visitation of Mary (Luke 1.39–56). In Gabriel's message to Mary, he informs her that her 'relative Elizabeth in her old age has also conceived a son' (Luke 1.36) after he has told her that she will bear Jesus.

From sources outside the canonical Gospels, we know that Mary's parents were recorded as Joachim and Anne. Perhaps Elizabeth was either a sister of Joachim or of Anne: we are not told.

Diagram
Family of John the Baptist (12)

Friends, Relations and Acquaintances of Jesus.

The Gospel writers were largely concerned with recording as much as possible that would point men and women to Jesus as the Messiah. (See *Evangelists*) Personal detail is sometimes frustratingly lacking because it was never the intention of the writers to create tidy, finely detailed biographies of Jesus, his family, and his friends. The personal detail contained in the Gospels is there for a particular purpose, and is never gratuitous. Many characters are fleeting and unknown and unnamed. Indeed, Peter's mother-in-law, though undoubtedly well known to Jesus, is not mentioned by name, and neither is Peter's wife. It is worth noting those who are named.

Andrew

A disciple of Jesus and the brother of Simon Peter. Indeed, according to John 1.41, 42 it was he who introduced Peter to Jesus.
(see *Disciples of Jesus*)

Anna

A widow of eighty-four, who appeared briefly on the scene at the Presentation of Jesus in the Temple. 'There was also a prophet, Anna the daughter of Phanuel, of the tribe of Asher' (Luke 2.36a).

Bartholomew

(see *Nathanael* below and *Disciples of Jesus*)

Bartimaeus

Bartimaeus – i.e. the son of Timaeus – was the blind man who accosted Jesus with the words 'Jesus, Son of David, have mercy on me!' (Mark 10.47) as Jesus and his disciples were leaving Jericho.

Cephas

This Hebrew nickname 'the rock' was given by Jesus to Simon, brother of Andrew (John 1.42). (Peter is the Greek translation of Cephas.)
(see *Peter* below and *Disciples of Jesus*)

Cleopas

One of Jesus' disciples, though not one of the Twelve. He is mentioned only at the end of Luke's Gospel, on the road to Emmaus. 'Then one of them, whose name was Cleopas, answered him, "Are you the only stranger in Jerusalem who does not know the things that have taken place there in these days"' (Luke 24.18).

Clopas

We know of Clopas only because he is mentioned in order to distinguish his wife, Mary, from the others at the cross of Jesus. Some have suggested that he was a brother of Joseph, Jesus' guardian. 'Meanwhile, standing near the cross of Jesus were his mother [Mary], and his mother's sister [Salome], Mary the wife of Clopas [Mary], and Mary Magdalene [Mary]' (John 19.25).
(see *Brothers of Jesus*, and *Women at the Cross*)

39

Friends, Relations and Acquaintances of Jesus

Elizabeth
The mother of John the Baptist and a relative of Mary, the mother of Jesus. As Elizabeth was 'getting on in years' (Luke 1.7) she may have died during Jesus' infancy.
(see *Family of John the Baptist*)

Jairus
Described as 'a leader of the synagogue' (Luke 8.41) whose daughter was gravely ill when he begged Jesus to heal her.

James I
This James – often called 'the Great' - was the one of the sons of Zebedee and Salome. He was a cousin of Jesus and member of the 'inner circle' of disciples (Luke 8.51), nicknamed with his brother, John, 'Sons of Thunder' by Jesus (Mark 3.17).
(see *Disciples of Jesus*)

James II
The second James of the disciples of Jesus was James, the son of Alphaeus and brother of Matthew (Luke 6.15).
(see *Disciples of Jesus*)

James III
This other James was the son of Mary, wife of Clopas, brother of Joseph (Joses) and others. He was probably James 'the Less', who became the leader of the church in Jerusalem (Mark 15.41; Acts 21.17, 18).
(see *Brothers of Jesus*)

Joanna
'The wife of Herod's steward Chuza' (Luke 8.3) and a follower of Jesus who helped provide for him during his ministry. She was one of those who took spices to the tomb (Luke 24.10).
(see *Women at the Cross*)

John
The most senior John was the father of Andrew and Simon Peter (John 1.42). He is not mentioned in any other context.

John the Baptist
We do not know much about the relationship of John with Jesus. He was, of course, a relative of Jesus (see *Elizabeth* above). Clearly Jesus had drawn disciples from John after John had pointed them in Jesus' direction (John 1.35–42).
(see *Essenes*)

John
John was one of the sons of Zebedee, and brother of James I (see *James I* above). He is quite reasonably identified with 'the disciple whom Jesus loved' of the Gospel of John (John 21.20).
(see *Disciples of Jesus*)

Joseph of Arimathea

This Joseph was a secret disciple of Jesus 'because of his fear of the Jews' (John 19.38). It was he who asked Pilate if he might remove the body of Jesus for burial.

Joseph Barsabbas

We know little of this Joseph except that he was selected as one of the two candidates for the position in the Twelve vacated by Judas Iscariot. In the event, Matthias was chosen. Clearly, Joseph had been a faithful and, probably, fairly close disciple of Jesus. '"So one of the men who have accompanied us throughout the time that the Lord went in and out among us, beginning from the baptism of John until the day he was taken up from us – one of these must become a witness with us to his resurrection." So they proposed two, Joseph called Barsabbas, who was also known as Justus, and Matthias' (Acts 1.21–23).

Joseph, Guardian of Jesus

The husband of Mary, the mother of Jesus, he is presented to us in the first two chapters of Matthew's and Luke's Gospels. There we are given some insight into his character and person. It was he whom the angel warned about Herod's murderous intentions. (Matthew 2.13–15) After these nativity narratives, nothing is heard of Joseph except when the hearers ask themselves in astonishment: 'Is not this Joseph's son?' (Luke 4.22) Mark's Gospel does not mention him but John's Gospel uses Joseph to help identify Jesus to Nathanael (John 1.45) and the Jews ask themselves: 'Is not this Jesus, the son of Joseph, whose father and mother we know?' (John 6.42) (see *Brothers of Jesus*)

Joseph (Joses)

This Joseph was the brother of James III and, probably, of Simon and Judas (Jude). His mother was Mary, the wife of Clopas (Matthew 27.56; John 19.25). It is possible that he replaced his brother James as the leader of the church in Jerusalem. (see *Brothers of Jesus*)

Judas (Jude)

This Judas was the brother of James III and of Joseph and Simon (Mark 6.3). It is feasible that he was the writer of the Letter of Jude, who prefaces the work with the words: 'Jude, a servant of Jesus Christ and brother of James, to those . . .' (Jude 1.1). (see *Brothers of Jesus*)

Judas Iscariot

One of the Twelve, and the one who betrayed Jesus. (see *Disciples of Jesus*)

Judas (not Iscariot)

We hear little of this Judas in the Gospels. He was one of the Twelve, the son of James (Luke 6.16) and probably identical with Thaddaeus in the Gospels of Matthew and Mark. In John 14.22 he asks: 'Lord, how is it that you will reveal yourself to us, and not to the world?' (see *Disciples of Jesus*)

Friends, Relations and Acquaintances of Jesus

Lazarus
A friend of Jesus, and brother of Martha and Mary. It is possible that they were the children of Simon the Leper (Matthew 26.6; Mark 14). Strangely, though Martha and Mary are mentioned in all four Gospels, Lazarus appears only in John where the miracle of his being brought back to life in John 11 is treated at length and with great care by the writer. Not only is the miracle of utmost significance as a foreshadowing of the Resurrection of Jesus (though Lazarus was to die again and Jesus rose from the dead to die no more) it is also one of the reasons why the Pharisees were determined that Jesus himself should die (John 11.45–54).

Levi
The tax-collector who, in response to Jesus' request, 'got up, left everything, and followed him' (Luke 5.28; Mark 2.14). In the Gospel of Matthew we have the same story, but here the man's name is Matthew (Matthew 9.9). It is likely that Jesus renamed Levi because, in Luke for example, even though the tax-collector is named Levi in Luke 5, by the time we reach the list of disciples in Luke 6.12-16, Matthew has appeared, but there is no Levi.

(see *Disciples of Jesus*)

Martha
The sister of Mary and of Lazarus and, possibly, the daughter of Simon the Leper (Mark 14.3; John 11.1, 2). Martha and her sister Mary are featured in all four Gospels. It was Martha's complaint to Jesus about her sister's apparent sloth that elicited from Jesus: 'Martha, Martha, you are worried and distracted by many things; there is need of only one thing. Mary has chosen the better part, which will not be taken away from her' (Luke 10.41).

Mary of Bethany
The sister of Martha and of Lazarus. She is clearly identified by the writer of John's Gospel as the one who anointed Jesus with precious ointment (John 11.1, 2). Mary was a devoted follower of Jesus, 'who sat at the Lord's feet and listened to what he was saying' (Luke 10.39).

Mary Magdalene
Although there has been a long tradition of associating this Mary with the woman whose sins were forgiven by Jesus, in the house of Simon the Pharisee, there is no real reason to connect the two except that the story is contained at the end of Luke 7, and Mary Magdalene is first mentioned at the beginning of the next chapter. Jesus says to Simon the Pharisee: 'Therefore, I tell you, her sins, which were many, have been forgiven', and Luke describes Mary five verses later as 'Mary, called Magdalene, from whom seven demons had gone out' (Luke 7.47; 8.2).

In view of the beginning of chapter 8 of Luke's Gospel, we know that Mary was a faithful follower of Jesus throughout his ministry. She features in the Resurrection narratives of all four Gospels but the Gospel of John records the most personal encounter when she 'saw Jesus standing there, but she did not know that it was Jesus. Jesus said to her, "Mary!" She turned and said to him in Hebrew, "Rabouni!" (which means Teacher)' (John 20.14–16).

(see *Women at the Cross*)

Mary, Mother of Jesus

Mary is mentioned in Matthew's nativity narrative only from the point of view of Joseph. Luke's nativity narratives take us from Gabriel's announcement to Mary (Luke 1.26–38), to the shepherds on the hillside (Luke 2.8–20), and on to the Finding in the Temple (Luke 2.41–52) and suggest that the source of this material at some stage in the writing of the Gospel was Mary herself.

Mary features little in the Gospels after the nativity narratives though she was with Jesus at the wedding in Cana (John 2.1–12) and, again, it is left to the writer of John to record the touching instruction from the mouth of Jesus from the cross; when he saw 'the disciple whom he loved standing beside her, he said to his mother, "Woman, here is your son" Then he said to the disciple, "Here is your mother."' (John 19.26, 27).

We can hardly doubt that Mary was present among 'the eleven and their companions gathered together . . . saying, "The Lord has risen indeed, and he has appeared to Simon!"' (Luke 24.33, 34), but we do know from Luke's Acts of the Apostles that after the Ascension, 'All these were constantly devoting themselves to prayer, together with certain women, including Mary the mother of Jesus' (Acts 1.14).
(see *Family of Jesus* and *Women at the Cross*)

Mary, Wife of Clopas

Although Mary, the wife of Clopas is so mentioned only by the writer of John (John 19.25), it is likely that she was also Mary 'the mother of James' (Luke 24.10), 'the mother of James the younger and of Joses [Joseph]' (Mark 15.40), and 'the other Mary' (Matthew 28.1). This Mary is quite likely to have been the mother of 'James and Joseph [Joses] and Simon and Judas' (Matthew 13.55). (Rather than constructing an accurate family tree, the writer is probably only allowing the people in the synagogue to say that they know where Jesus comes from and who his relations are.)
(see *Brothers of Jesus* and *Women at the Cross*)

Matthew

Matthew seems to have been the name given to Levi by Jesus.
(see *Levi* above, and *Disciples of Jesus*)

Matthias

We know little of Matthias except that he was selected as one of the two candidates for the position in the Twelve vacated by Judas Iscariot. In the event, Matthias was chosen. Clearly, he had been a faithful and, probably, fairly close disciple of Jesus. '"So one of the men who have accompanied us throughout the time that the Lord went in and out among us, beginning from the baptism of John until the day he was taken up from us – one of these must become a witness with us to his resurrection." So they proposed two, Joseph called Barsabbas, who was also known as Justus, and Matthias. And they cast lots for them, and the lot fell on Matthias; and he was added to the eleven apostles' (Acts 1.21–23, 26).

Nathanael

The Nathanael included as one of Jesus' disciples in the Gospel of John is almost certainly one and the same with the Bartholomew noted in the Gospels of Matthew, Mark and Luke. After all, Bartholomew is merely a surname – the son of Tolmai. 'Philip found Nathanael and said to him, "We have found him about whom Moses

Friends, Relations and Acquaintances of Jesus

in the law and also the prophets wrote, Jesus son of Joseph from Nazareth." Nathanael said to him, "Can anything good come out of Nazareth?" Philip said to him, "Come and see."' (John 1.45, 46).
(see *Disciples of Jesus*)

Nicodemus

A Pharisee and 'a leader of the Jews' (John 3.1) and, perhaps, on the fringes of those who followed Jesus. He it was who assisted Joseph of Arimathea with the burying of Jesus in the sepulchre and provided 'a mixture of myrrh and aloes, weighing about a hundred pounds' (John 19.39).

Peter

Peter, one of the 'inner circle' of Jesus' disciples, was introduced to Jesus by Andrew. 'He first found his brother Simon and said to him, "We have found the Messiah" (which is translated 'Anointed'). He brought Simon to Jesus, who looked at him and said, "You are Simon son of John. You are to be called Cepha"' (which is translated Peter)' (John 1.41, 42).
(see *Disciples of Jesus*)

Philip

Philip was one of Jesus' disciples and, according to the Gospel of John, was recruited by Jesus in Galilee. 'He found Philip and said to him, "Follow me." Now Philip was from Bethsaida, the city of Andrew and Peter' (John 1.43, 44).
(see *Disciples of Jesus*)

Salome

The wife of Zebedee and sister of Mary, the mother of Jesus. She was the mother of the disciples James and John (two members of the 'inner circle' of disciples) and requested that Jesus should: 'Declare that these two sons of mine will sit, one at your right hand and one at your left, in your kingdom' (Matthew 20.21). Salome was one of the women 'looking on from a distance' at the Crucifixion of Jesus (Mark 15.40) and, presumably, one of those who 'saw the tomb and how his body was laid' (Luke 23.55) and one of those who carried spices and saw the empty tomb (Mark 16.1 and Luke 24.1–11).
(see *Brothers of Jesus, Family of Jesus* and *Women at the Cross*)

Simeon

The old man who met Jesus in infancy and 'took him in his arms and praised God, saying, ". . . my eyes have seen your salvation, which you have prepared in the presence of all peoples, a light for the revelation to the Gentiles and for glory to your people Israel"' on the occasion of Jesus' Presentation in the Temple (Luke 2.22–35).

Simon

This Simon is mentioned only in Matthew 13.55 – 'And are not his brothers James and Joseph and Simon and Judas?' and in Mark 6.3. Whether or not these brothers were in fact uterine brothers of Jesus is open to question.
(see *Brothers of Jesus*)

Simon of Cyrene

The Gospel of John does not record Jesus' journey from Gabbatha (the place of sentence) to Golgotha (the place of crucifixion) except to say: 'and carrying the cross by himself, he went out'. The other Gospels record that along the way Jesus was unable cope with the weight of the cross, and so the soldiers 'compelled a passer-by, who was coming in from the country, to carry his cross; it was Simon of Cyrene, the father of Alexander and Rufus' (Mark 15.21).

Simon the Leper

This man was, possibly, the father of Mary and Lazarus (Mark 14.3 and John 11.1, 2). (see *Martha, Mary* and *Lazarus* above)

Simon Peter

Simon, surnamed Peter (the rock) by Jesus, was the brother of Andrew. With James and John, he was of the 'inner circle' of the disciples. It was Simon Peter who declared to Jesus: 'You are the Messiah' in response to which Jesus revealed that Peter was being groomed as the leader of the Church. 'Blessed are you, Simon son of Jonah! For flesh and blood has not revealed this to you, but my father in heaven. And I tell you, you are Peter, and on this rock I will build my church, and the gates of Hades will not prevail against it. I will give you the keys of the kingdom of heaven' (Matthew 16.16–19).
(see *Disciples of Jesus*)

Simon the Pharisee

Some scholars confuse or identify Simon the Pharisee with Simon the Leper. It is true that the story in Luke 7.36–50 shares some superficial similarities with the story of the anointing of Jesus by Mary of Bethany: in the house of Simon the Pharisee, however, we are clearly in the house of an acquaintance rather than a close friend.

Simon the Zealot (or the Canaanite)

This disciple was, or had been, a member of the more extreme wing of Judaism. His name is contained in the list of the Twelve in the Gospels of Matthew, Mark and Luke, and at the beginning of Acts.
(see *Disciples of Jesus*)

Susanna

One of the many 'who provided for them [Jesus and the disciples] out of their resources' (Luke 8.3). It is not unreasonable to suggest that she may have numbered among those 'who had followed him from Galilee and who watched the Crucifixion at a distance' (Luke 23.49).

Thaddaeus

(see *Judas (not Iscariot)* above)

Thomas

It was Thomas who urged his fellow disciples 'Let us also go, [to Judea] that we may die with him [Jesus]' (John 11.16).
(see *Disciples of Jesus*)

Zacchaeus

A rich (and crooked) tax-collector who, anxious to catch a glimpse of Jesus, climbed into a sycamore tree. Jesus called to him and told him 'I must stay at your house today.'· So he hurried down and was happy to welcome him' (Luke 19.5, 6). Luke tells us that Zacchaeus resolved to pay restitution to all those he had defrauded, and records Jesus' words 'Today salvation has come to this house, because he too is a son of Abraham' (Luke 19.9).

Zebedee

The husband of Salome, and father of James and John.
(see *Salome* above, and *Disciples of Jesus*)

Zechariah

The husband of Elizabeth, and father of John the Baptist.
(see *Elizabeth* above, and *Family of John the Baptist*)

Gad, Tribe of

Gad was the seventh son of Jacob, the first by Leah's servant Zilpah, and thus the ancestor of the tribe of Gad. 'Then Leah's maid Zilpah bore Jacob a son. And Leah said, "Good fortune!" so she named him Gad' (Genesis 30.10, 11). The land allocated to the Gadites, according to Joshua 18.7b and 22.1–9, was the highland east of the Jordan between the tribal land of Reuben and that of the eastern part of the Josephite tribe of Manasseh.

Diagrams
Children of Israel (3)
Tribal Lands of Israel (8)

Gentiles

Strictly speaking, Gentiles are those who belong to a nation; those who have a specific national identity; those who can be identified as a nation. Perhaps 'a people' is the best translation, if this meaning is to be conveyed. 'Now the Lord said to Abram, "Go from your country and your kindred and your father's house to the land that I will show you. I will make of you a great *nation*"' (Genesis 12.1, 2) and 'When they came to Jesus, they appealed to him earnestly, saying, "He is worthy of having you do this for him, for he loves our *people*"' (Luke 7.4, 5).

More commonly, the terms *gôy* (Hebrew) and *ethnos* (Greek) are translated as 'Gentiles' and used to denote non-Hebrews (Old Testament) and non-Jews (New Testament), often in the widest sense of 'the rest of the world'. At first, the Gentiles were merely those of the countries surrounding the infant nation of Israel – those who worshipped other gods, for example. As the God of Israel came to be seen as the God of all peoples, the Gentiles were, therefore, those who worshipped nothing other than idols. And yet, in the New Testament, Gentiles are sometimes simply those who do not know how to worship God properly. 'When you are praying, do not heap up empty phrases as the Gentiles do; for they think that they will be heard because of their many words' (Matthew 6.7). Nevertheless, Isaiah saw that the God of Israel was the God of all nations and that 'Many peoples shall come and say, "Come, let us go up to the mountain of the Lord, to the house of the God of Jacob; that he may teach us his ways and that we may walk in his paths"' (Isaiah 2.3). And the mission of the Messiah was summed up by Simeon as he held the infant Jesus in his arms 'and praised God, saying, ". . . for my eyes have seen your salvation, which you have prepared in the presence of all peoples, a light for revelation to the Gentiles and for glory to your people Israel"' (Luke 2.28–32).

Geshurites

A tribe of Arameans who lived, along with the tribe of Maacathites in the land allocated to the tribe of Manasseh. Even in King David's day, they were self-governing and were ruled by a king (Joshua 12.5).
(see *Maacathites*)

Diagram
Map of the Fertile Crescent (5)

Gibeonites

The inhabitants of the city of Gibeon in the territory of Benjamin, and north of Jerusalem. Shrewdly, they entered into a peace treaty with the Israelites in order to avoid a clash with Joshua's forces. They were condemned to a life in service to the Israelites; they were to be 'slaves, hewers of wood and drawers of water' (Joshua 9.23). However, the Gibeonites assisted with Nehemiah's reconstruction of the walls of Jerusalem. (Nehemiah 3.7)
(see *People of the Captivity and Return*)

Diagram
Map of Canaan (6)

Gileadites

The inhabitants of Gilead, north of the Dead Sea and east of the Jordan. Their land was taken by the Israelites when King Sihon of the Amorites was defeated (Numbers 21.24–26). An Israelite clan of the Gileadites is implied in the Song of Deborah (Judges 5.17) but this may be simply a reference to the Israelites who were happy to settle in the land of Gilead, east of the Jordan.

Diagram
Map of Canaan (6)

Girgashites

One of the many races found by the Israelites in the land of Canaan (Joshua 3.10). However, according to Genesis 10.15–18, Canaan, the son of Ham and the grandson of Noah, was responsible for fathering all the races that Canaan contained.

Gospel Writers

(see *Evangelists*)

Greeks, Grecians and Hellenists

Even though there are minor conflicts among the different translations of the Bible, generally speaking, *Greeks* are those of Greek descent but, occasionally, the word is used as a synonym for Gentiles (see *Gentiles)*. The use of *Greeks* for Gentiles is not difficult to understand in the context of the legacy of Alexander the Great's conquests, because the whole of what most people recognized as the world – certainly *their* world – was Greek-speaking. *Grecians* and *Hellenists*, more often than not, are the terms used to describe Greek-speaking Jews of the Diaspora (see *Diaspora*).

By the time the Persians had conquered Babylonia and moved westwards around the Fertile Crescent, spreading south into Egypt and Libya and west to Ephesus, the Persian Empire's eastern boundary reached as far as India and the lands of the Scythians. The Persian Empire flourished for about two hundred years, from 538 BC to 331 BC. This was the stage made ready for the appearance of Alexander the Great, the son of Philip of Macedon and pupil of Aristotle, and a man who became skilled in conquest and battle, and who believed passionately in establishing the culture and learning of ancient Greece throughout the world of his Empire. By the time of his death in 323 BC – he was not even thirty-three – he had conquered the lands embraced by the Persian Empire to the very banks of the Indus. On his death, his Empire was divided among his generals. Of those generals, Seleucus controlled Syria and Mesopotamia from his capital at Antioch, and Ptolemy Egypt and, at first, Palestine, from his capital at Alexandria, the city named after Alexander.

The Hellenistic culture (from *Hellas*, the ancient name for Greece) about which Alexander was so passionate, was enthusiastically propagated and developed in both the Seleucid and Ptolemaic Empires: harshly in the former, benignly in the latter. But it was Alexandria, which became the more significant of the two capitals in terms of art, culture and learning. The Hellenization of these two parts of the former Alexandrian Empire was swift, aided by the rapid spread of *koine* Greek throughout the eastern Mediterranean and beyond.

Koine Greek was a development of the common language of the Greeks and the lingua franca of the Hellenized countries – in Egypt, for example, *koine* Greek was adopted by the Aramaic-speaking Jewish community. Indeed, during the first half of the third century BC was completed in Alexandria, the translation of Jewish scripture into Greek – the Septuagint.

The Ptolemaic rule over Palestine came to an end in 198 BC when Antiochus III, the Syrian king, wrested the region from Ptolemy V. The Seleucids were fanatical and ruthless Hellenizers and, under their rule, stimulated by the desecration of the temple with the erection of an altar to Zeus, Israel revolted under the Maccabees. Judas Maccabeus won an unlikely advantage over the Syrians in 165 BC, which allowed the Jews to enjoy autonomy of the region for one hundred years, until the Roman Empire reached Jerusalem in the person of Pompey in 63 BC. The language of *koine* Greek remained the language of those around the eastern Mediterranean throughout the Roman era, and it was in this language that the Gospel was preached and the New Testament written, allowing the Christian message to travel rapidly beyond Judea and Galilee and throughout the Roman Empire.
(see *Writers of the Old Testament*)

Gutians

A people who entered into Mesopotamia from the north-east and effectively brought
Akkadian supremacy to an end in about 2180 BC.
(see *Akkadians*)

Habiru, or Hapiru

The Habiru are first mentioned in the eighteenth-century BC tablets found at Mari, a
city between present-day Syria and present-day Iraq. This was the period of
Hammurabi, *c*.1728–*c*.1686 BC, the greatest king of the first Babylonian Era. The
people of this Babylonian Empire were the Amorites, semi-nomads from the
Arabian Desert, who had opportunistically overrun Mesopotamia during the
collapse of the great Sumerian kingdom based around Ur. The cause of this collapse
was the invasion by the Elamites from the mountains beyond Mesopotamia, in
present-day Iran.

Ur, incidentally, was Abraham's ancestral home, and the migration of his family
– around 1750 BC – to Haran, and eventually to Canaan, was probably associated
with the general movements of many peoples during this period. 'Terah took his son
Abram and his grandson Lot son of Haran, and his daughter-in-law Sarai, his son
Abram's wife, and they went out from Ur of the Chaldeans to go to the land of
Canaan; but when they came to Haran, they settled there' (Genesis 11.31). It is worth
noting how often the names of cities throughout Mesopotamia correspond with the
names of members of Abraham's family.

But who were the Habiru? It seems likely, though all scholars do not agree, that
there was a close connection between the Hebrews and the Habiru. However, one
cannot necessarily be identified with the other. The second millennium BC references
to the Habiru apparently refer to *any* wandering people, as opposed to those who
lived in a settled state or nation. (Certainly, the Hebrews were, from time to time in
their early existence, a wandering people. Abraham's family trekked from Ur to
Haran and into Canaan; his descendants settled in Egypt, forced from Canaan by
famine; and, following the Exodus from Egypt, wandered the wilderness for years
before finally subduing most of Canaan.) Probably, the term *Habiru* was, at first,
applied to no more than the gypsy-like bands of travellers who lived on the fringes
of established society, and only gradually applied, as a generic term, to all types of
nomads and semi-nomads, among whom the Hebrews most assuredly numbered,
during long periods of their early existence.

Diagrams
Descent of Abraham (1)
Family of Abraham (2)
Broad Parallel Histories (17)

Hagrites or Hagarites, Hagarenes, Hagarens

At one time it was thought that the Hagrites were, perhaps, the descendants of Hagar,
and, therefore, synonymous with the Ishmaelites. More likely, they were distinct
from the Ishmaelites, an Aramean tribe, perhaps, that had settled on land east of
Gilead. '. . . *the tents of Edom and the Ishmaelites, Moab and the Hagrites*' (Psalm
83.6). 'And in the days of Saul they made war on the Hagrites, who fell by their hand;

and they lived in their tents throughout all the region east of Gilead' (1 Chronicles 5.10).

Hamathites

The last-mentioned of the descendant families of Noah's grandson, Canaan (Genesis 10.18). Hamath was a small kingdom sitting on the northern border of Solomon's Israel.

Hamites

Ham was the second son of Noah and thus the father of all the Canaanite and Cushite peoples – the Hamites. The Noah stories give us a picture of a world peopled, in one way or another, by the descendants of Noah, and show the cause of the enmity between the descendants of Ham's son, Canaan (the Canaanites), and those of Noah's son, Shem (the Semites) (Genesis 10). The cursing of Canaan does, however, suggest that one tradition held that Canaan was Noah's son, not his grandson, otherwise Noah would surely have cursed Ham!

Diagram
Descent of Abraham (1)

Hasideans

A Judean group of the early second century BC who resisted Hellenization under Antiochus IV. From time to time they assisted and formed a coalition with the Hasmoneans in order to enforce, sometimes brutally, the letter of Jewish law. 'Then there united with them a company of Hasideans, mighty warriors of Israel, all who offered themselves willingly for the law' (1 Maccabees 2.42). The Hasideans probably gave rise to the Pharisaic party of New Testament times, and, possibly to the party of the Essenes, though the latter were a somewhat more contemplative group. (see *Essenes* and *Pharisees*)

Hasmoneans or Hasadim

Another name for the Maccabees. Although Mattathias was the founder of the Maccabean dynasty, he was himself a descendant of Hasmon, from a priestly but non-Aaronic family (1 Maccabees 2.1–6).
(see *Maccabees*)

Hebrews, Israelites, Jews

The descendants of the family of Abraham who, through Jacob (Israel) became the children of Israel, the Israelites. It may be that the term derives from the name of Abraham's ancestor, Eber (Genesis 10.21–31).

The terms 'Hebrews' and 'Israelites' often appear interchangeable although, sometimes, the first seems to be used by non-Israelites in order to refer to the second, and by the second when referring to themselves in conversation with non-Israelites. In Roman times, all those who practised the religion of the Israelites, and those who inhabited the Province of Judea were called Jews. This province was, broadly speaking, the old kingdom of Judah.

Those to whom the anonymous New Testament letter, *The Letter to the Hebrews*, is addressed were likely to have been Christians with a Jewish background. However, this is by no means certain because the title was added after the letter had begun to circulate.

(see *Children of Israel* and *Habiru*)

Diagrams
Descent of Abraham (1)
Family of Abraham (2)
Children of Israel (3)

Hellenists

(see *Greeks*)

Herodians

A political party yearning for the re-establishment of the kingdom of Israel under the Herodian dynasty. In the New Testament, they seem to be closely associated with the Pharisees. 'The Pharisees went out and immediately conspired with the Herodians against him [Jesus], how to destroy him' (Mark 3.6). 'Then they sent to him some Pharisees and some Herodians to trap him [Jesus] in what he said' (Mark 12.13).

Herods

Herod the Great
The Hasmoneans flourished towards the end of the Seleucid period of influence in Palestine, up to the time Rome began to take a greater interest in the most eastern corner of its growing empire. They had wrested control of Palestine from the Seleucids and now the Hasmoneans were clearly not going to be able to cope, philosophically, with any form of imperial domination. The stage was set for political expediency, and Herod the Great.

The Herodian dynasty was popular as it gave some semblance of an independent Jewish state, but by the time of Herod the Great's death in 4 BC, Rome was ready to take full control of the region. However, Herod had impressed Rome immensely – he had been much more than a mere 'puppet' king – and, for the most part, Rome found in his sons a useful buffer between the people and the authority of Rome. And Herod the Great had had a distinct advantage in establishing himself as king in the eyes of the Jewish people, in that through his second wife, Mariamne, (there were two so named among his ten wives) he had married into the Hasmonean family. She was the granddaughter of Hyrcanus II. Not that that had prevented Herod's having her uncle, Antigonus II, murdered, with a little help from Rome. Greed, immorality and expediency seem to have been the building blocks of the Herodian dynasty. That Herod the Great was an Idumean (an Edomite) did not endear him to everyone. (His father was an Idumean and his mother a Nabatean.) The Edomites (the descendants of Esau) had only lately been classed under Deuteronomic Law as 'brother' though Edom had, in fact, fallen under Judah's control, and had been effectively taken into his kingdom by King David himself.

Herod the Great is featured throughout the second chapter of Matthew's Gospel. He it was who was consulted by the wise men; he it was who, after seeking advice, asked the wise men to inform him of Jesus' whereabouts; he it was who instigated the murder of 'all the children in and around Bethlehem who were two years old or under, according to the time that he had learned from the wise men' (Matthew 2.16). (see *Idumeans* and *Nabateans*)

Archelaus

The son of Herod the Great and his fourth wife, Malthace, a Samaritan, and was, until AD 6, ethnarch of Judea, Samaria and Idumea. It was Archelaus whom Mary and Joseph wished to avoid when they left their period of exile in Egypt, and so took up residence in Nazareth (Matthew 2.19–23).

Herod Antipas

The full brother of Archelaus and, until AD 39, tetrarch of Galilee and Perea. It was this Herod who was roundly condemned by John the Baptist for marrying Herodias, his half brother's wife (Luke 3.18–20). And it was to Herod Antipas that Pilate sent Jesus during his trials. (Luke 23.6–12).

Herod Philip

The son of Herod the Great and Mariamne, Herod the Great's third wife, the second Mariamne. It was Herod Philip's wife who left him for Herod Antipas.

Philip the Tetrarch

This Philip was the ruler of Iturea and the son of Herod the Great and Cleopatra, Herod the Great's fifth wife. Philip married Salome, the daughter of his half brother Herod Philip and Herodias.

Herod Agrippa I

Agrippa I was well thought of by Rome and by the Jews. He was the grandson of Herod the Great and the first Mariamne, Herod the Great's second wife. It was Agrippa I who 'had James, the brother of John, killed with the sword. After he saw that it pleased the Jews, he proceeded to arrest Peter also' (Acts 1. 2, 3).

Herod Agrippa II

Before Agrippa II, the son of Agrippa I, Paul defended himself against certain charges brought by the Jews. 'Agrippa said to Paul, "You have permission to speak for yourself." Then Paul stretched out his hand and began to defend himself: "I consider myself fortunate that it is before you, King Agrippa, I am to make my defence today"' (Acts 26.1, 2).

Felix

The governor of Judea who, though not of the Herodian dynasty himself, was connected to it by virtue of the fact that he was the second husband of Drusilla, the great granddaughter of Herod the Great and the first Mariamne. He left Paul languishing in prison for two years before his successor as governor – Porcius Festus – took Paul to Agrippa II.
(see *Hasmoneans* and *Maccabees*)

Diagram
Tree of Herod the Great (11)

Hittites

'Every place that the sole of your foot will tread upon I have given to you, as I promised to Moses. From the wilderness and the Lebanon as far as the great river, the river Euphrates, all the land of the Hittites, to the Great Sea in the west shall be your territory' (Joshua 1.3, 4). By the time the Israelites were looking across the Jordan deciding on the likely extent of their task, the Hittite empire was in decline. However, the Hittites referred to here were, probably, those refugees or emigrants from the empire who had settled in Canaan: the empire had never extended as far south as the land of Canaan.

The empire of the Hittites had developed from the city kingdoms of Asia Minor (largely, modern-day Turkey) in about 1800 BC. Historians and scholars have sometimes identified one of the earliest known Hittite kings – Tudhaliyas – as Tidal of Goiim mentioned in Genesis 14.1. Of that we cannot be certain. But by about 1600 BC the empire had extended south into northern Aram (Syria) and around 1560 BC the Hittites raided Babylon, which ultimately brought about the end of the First Babylonian Empire.

The first half of the fourteenth century BC saw the flowering of the Hittites, the period of a new Hittite empire. The Hittites now held sway over the Mitanni of Upper Mesopotamia (who had been, incidentally, the greatest power in the region between 1500 BC and the end of the fourteenth century BC) and now extended as far south as Lebanon. Here the empire came into direct contact with Egypt when, at the time of Rameses II, Egypt had a reasonable degree of control over Canaan in that the inhabitants of Canaan would not consider causing Egypt any trouble because they were busy enough arguing among themselves. Inevitably there was conflict between Egypt and the Hittites, most famously, at Kadesh in 1297 BC. The battle was described by Rameses as a triumph in the great victory carvings of the time, but was probably no more than an indecisive skirmish. However, it brought about a prudent peace-treaty under which the two sides agreed that the river Orontes was the common boundary between the two empires. Rameses II even added a Hittite princess to his collection of wives.

This new Hittite empire was in decline about 1200 BC with the rise of Assyria and by succumbing to attacks from the west. Thereafter it seems to have returned, in form, to a series of about seven city kingdoms, the last of which were the independent kingdoms of Hamath and Carchemish, which were conquered by Sargon II of the re-emerging Assyria in 720 BC and 717 BC respectively. (Carchemish was the site of the battle in 605 BC when the Babylonians defeated the Egyptian army.) (see *Assyrians, Babylonians and Mitannians*)

Diagrams
Map of the Fertile Crescent (5)
Broad Parallel Histories (17, 18)

Hivites

One of the many races or peoples the Israelites absorbed or displaced in Canaan. 'So the Israelites lived among the Canaanites, the Hittites, the Amorites, the Perizzites, the Hivites, and the Jebusites; and they took their daughters as wives for themselves, and their own daughters they gave to their sons; and they worshipped their gods' (Judges 3.5, 6). Their land seems to have been the area between the river Litani and the river Hasbani in Lebanon. Like the Amorites, they may have been the remnant of a once great people displaced from another region. They were of non-Semitic origin. (see *Shechemites*)

Holy Family

This is the title usually given to Jesus, Mary and Joseph.
(see *Family of Jesus*)

Horites

In all probability, they were Hurrians who had pressed forward into Canaan during the expansion of the Mitanni kingdom. Some had settled 'in the hill country of Seir as far as El-paran on the edge of the wilderness' (Genesis 14.6). They were, therefore, predecessors of the Edomites.
(see *Hittites, Hurrians* and *Mitannians*)

Diagram
Map of the Fertile Crescent (5)

Hurrians

As the Amorites were pushing up to the Fertile Crescent from the Arabian Desert, the Hurrians were entering Mesopotamia at about Haran from Armenia, from the northern mountains between the Black and Caspian Seas. They spread slowly but surely, by insinuation rather than by conquest, throughout Mesopotamia and into Palestine. By the end of Hammurabi's reign, they comprised the majority of the inhabitants of what would become the Kingdom of Mitanni from the beginning of the fifteenth century until about thirty years into the fourteenth century BC, sandwiched in time between the Old Hittite Empire and the New. It is of interest that clay tablets from the Mitanni period reveal a Hurrian tradition reflected in Genesis 31.19–35, that ownership of household gods confirms headship of the family. It is clear that during this period of the Patriarchs' wanderings, influences from other peoples were of significance. The broad sweep of the Genesis saga occurred within great movements of peoples: the Patriarchs were very much a part of it, not aloof or separate from it.
(see *Habiru* and *Hittites*)

Diagram
Map of the Fertile Crescent (5)

Hyksos

The Hyksos began to penetrate Syria and Canaan during the beginning of the second millennium BC. They were mostly of West Semitic and Levantine origin, but it is believed that they may have included some Hittites and Hurrians. The name *Hyksos* is an Egyptian name for 'foreign rulers' or 'rulers of other lands' suggesting, perhaps, a mixture of races.

The Hyksos seem to have swept down into Egypt determined to conquer and to overthrow. There is, as yet, no evidence to support a popular belief that the Hyksos' superiority over Egypt was due to a great extent to the horse and chariot. It is likely, rather, that the invasion coincided with a period of extreme weakness in Egypt's political structure, just before 1700 BC. For about one hundred and fifty years the Hyksos ruled in Egypt – and, for that matter, in Canaan and Syria – with their capital established at Avaris in the Delta region. About 1570 BC the Hyksos were finally expelled after years of unrest and revolution in Egypt. Ahmose I then founded the eighteenth Dynasty.

This history gives us the backdrop of the descent of Jacob's family into Egypt after the Hyksos had established themselves. The Hebrews lived in harmony with the mainly Semitic rulers in Egypt but, after the expulsion of the Hyksos, the Egyptians' tolerance of the Hebrews waned until they were substantially enslaved. Probably around 1300–1290 BC, during the reign of Seti I and early in the reign of Rameses II, although there is still much argument as to the date, the Exodus was planned and executed.

(see *Hittites, Hurrians* and *Patriarchs*)

Diagrams
Map of the Fertile Crescent (5)
Broad Parallel Histories (17)

Idumeans

The inhabitants of the land south of Judea whose population was made up of a number of races, though Edomites were probably in the majority – hence the Greek name *Idumea,* meaning 'of the Edomites'. The land was so named during the Hellenistic period. Herod the Great was an Idumean.
(see *Edomites, Greeks* and *Herods*)

Ishmaelites

The descendants of Ishmael, the son of Abraham and his concubine, Hagar. Ishmael and his mother were cast out in favour of Isaac, the son of Abraham and Sarah. God told Abraham 'I will make a nation of him [Ishmael] also, because he is your offspring' (Genesis 21.13). The families of Ishmael's twelve sons settled in the wildernesses of Shur and Paran in the Arabian Desert (Genesis 25.12-18). Very few references to Ishmaelites appear in the Old Testament subsequently, though they are sometimes mentioned in association with or confusion with Midianites, as in the story of the rescue of Joseph. (Genesis 37.27, 28).The name *Ishmael* means 'May God hear' or 'May God be aware'. Tradition makes the Ishmaelites the antecedents of all Arabs.
(see *Family of Abraham*)

Diagram
Family of Abraham (2)

Israel, Tribes of

(see individual tribes: *Asher, Benjamin, Dan, Ephraim, Gad, Issachar, Joseph, Judah, Levi, Manasseh, Naphthali, Reuben, Simon, Zebulun*)

Diagram
Tribal Lands of Israel (8)

Israelites

(see *Children of Israel, Hebrews* and *Israel, Tribes of*)

Issachar, Tribe of

Issachar was the ninth son of Jacob and the fifth by Leah, and thus the ancestor of the tribe of Issachar. 'And God heeded Leah, and she conceived and bore Jacob a fifth son. Leah said, "God has given me my hire because I gave my maid to my husband"; so she named him Issachar' (Genesis 30.17, 18). The land allocated to the tribe, according to Joshua 19.17–23, was west of the Jordan below Galilee, and between the land of Zebulun and the western portion of the tribal land of Manasseh.

Diagrams
Children of Israel (3)
Tribal Lands of Israel (8)

Ithrites

Members of one of the families of the tribe of Judah living in Kiriath-jearim (1 Chronicles 2.53). Two of them 'Ira the Ithrite, Gareb the Ithrite' are named as members of David's bodyguard (2 Samuel 23.39).

James, Principal Individuals Named

Of the three individuals named James in the New Testament, two were disciples of Jesus and one is described as one of his brothers.
(see *Brothers of Jesus, Disciples of Jesus* and *Family of Jesus*)

Jebusites

According to Genesis 10.15–20, the Jebusites were one of the many tribes comprising the Canaanites, who descended from Canaan, the son of Ham and grandson of Noah. They were, consequently, among the many with whom the Israelites had to contend as they set about establishing themselves in Canaan (Exodus 3.17).

Jerahmeelites

Descendants of the family of Jerahmeel, a descendant of Judah (1 Chronicles 2.4, 9, 25–27, 33). They lived below the land of the tribe of Judah, on the edge of the Negeb. The land of the Jerahmeelites was probably a part of Judah by the time of David's kingship.

Jews

(see *Hebrews, Israelites, Jews*)

Joseph, Principal Individuals Named

Joseph (Joses)
(see *Brothers of Jesus* and *Friends, Relations and Acquaintances of Jesus*)

Joseph of Arimathea
(see *Friends, Relations and Acquaintances of Jesus*)

Joseph Barsabbas
(see *Friends, Relations and Acquaintances of Jesus*)

Joseph, Guardian of Jesus
The story of the Nativity of Jesus is told in the Gospels of Luke and Matthew. Luke's account concentrates upon the journey to Bethlehem so that Joseph and Mary can take part in the Roman census; Matthew's deals with Joseph's initial reluctance to take Mary as his wife, his escape with his family to Egypt, and his settling in Nazareth. (Luke 1, 2 and Matthew 1, 3) Outside these chapters Joseph is mentioned only in passing: it is assumed that he died before Jesus began his ministry.
(see *Friends, Relations and Acquaintances of Jesus*)

Joseph, son of Jacob
The eleventh son of Jacob and the first by Rachel. Largely through envy, his brothers plotted first to kill him, then to sell him into slavery. The band of merchants to whom he was sold, took him to Egypt and sold him to Potiphar, Pharaoh's captain of the guard. In Egypt, Joseph prospered and was promoted. He set aside food in anticipation of the famine to come, and his prudence allowed Egypt to provide for itself and, in addition, sell food to others suffering under the widespread famine. It was in these circumstances that Jacob, Joseph's father, ultimately journeyed with his sons and their families to Egypt (Genesis 37, 41, 42, 43–47).This is the story of how the Children of Israel (the Children of Jacob) came to settle in Egypt from the land of Canaan.

Diagrams
Children of Israel (3)
Tribal Lands of Israel (8)

Joseph, Tribe of

Joseph was the eleventh son of Jacob, and the first by Rachel. 'Then God remembered Rachel, and God heeded her and opened her womb. She conceived and bore a son, and said, "God has taken away my reproach"; and she named him Joseph, saying, "May the Lord add to me another son!" '(Genesis 30.22–24). Joseph had two sons – Manasseh and Ephraim – whom Jacob adopted, and thus they numbered with their uncles as ancestors of the tribes of Israel. The lands allocated to the tribe of Joseph were divided between the half tribe of Manasseh and that of Ephraim (Joshua 13.29–31; 14.1–4; 16; 17).

Diagrams
Children of Israel (3)
Tribal Lands of Israel (8)

Judah, Tribe of

Judah was the fourth son of Jacob and the fourth by Leah. 'She conceived again and bore a son, and said, "This time I will praise the Lord"; therefore she named him Judah; then she ceased bearing' (Genesis 29.35). He was the ancestor of the tribe of Judah and of the Nation. The territory of Judah was originally somewhat smaller than that noted in Joshua 15, which seems to outline the extent of the later kingdom of Judah.

Diagrams
Children of Israel (3)
Tribal Lands of Israel (8)

Judas, Principal Individuals Named

Judas (Jude)
(see *Brothers of Jesus* and *Family of Jesus*)

Judas Barsabbas
Mentioned in Acts 15.22, 23: 'Then the apostles and the elders, with the consent of the whole church, decided to choose men from among their members and to send them to Antioch with Paul and Barnabas. They sent Judas called Barsabbas, and Silas, leaders among the brothers, with the following letter . . .'

Judas Iscariot
(see *Disciples of Jesus*)

Judas Maccabeus
(see *Hasmoneans* and *Maccabees*)

Judas (not Iscariot)
(see *Disciples of Jesus*)

Judges

Heroes of the period in Israel's existence – roughly speaking, from 1200–1000 BC – between the entry into Canaan and the making of a nation under King Saul. The judges of Israel, according to the Book of Judges, were non-hereditary tribal leaders and chieftains who, it seems, arose in response to the problem of the moment. They were those with a God-given authority and ability to whom the tribe looked for crucial decisions. Only Gideon seems to have been offered the kingship of Israel, an honour he refused. Not until Samuel entered upon the scene was Israel able to move forward from a disparate collection of tribes that occasionally worked and fought with one another, first, to the idea of a united country under King Saul and, secondly, to the reality of a united country under David. Samuel, part prophet, part priest, part judge, part kingmaker, was the link between the two very different Israels.

Othniel
Saved Israel from the hand of King Cushan-rishathaim of Aram-naharaim, in the south country. Cushan had subjugated the people of Israel for eight years; after his death, 'the land had rest for forty years' (Judges 2.11).

Ehud

The son of the Benjaminite, Gera, and the second judge of Israel. He came to prominence after King Eglon of Moab 'in alliance with the Ammonites and the
Amalekites' had defeated Israel (Judges 3.13). For eighteen years 'the Israelites
served King Eglon of Moab' (Judges 3.14). Through a little clever deception, the
left-handed Ehud killed the fat King Eglon with a specially crafted sword.
Apparently, a period of eighty years' peace followed.

Shamgar

There is only a brief reference to this judge in Judges 3.31, although he is mentioned
later, in the Song of Deborah (Judges 5.6).

Shamgar was responsible for the elimination of six hundred Philistines. If *son of
Anath* means that he flourished in Beth-Anath in the north, perhaps he protected trad-
ing parties of Israelites from marauding Philistines, or attacked trading columns of
Philistines as they moved north from their land further down the coast.

Deborah

Referred to as both judge and prophetess. 'She used to sit under the palm of Deborah
between Ramah and Bethel in the hill country of Ephraim' (Judges 4.5). The
Canaanites had oppressed Israel for twenty years, and against this background,
Deborah's army under her general Barak, defeated the Canaanites. Victory was
sweetened yet further in the two accounts – subtly different in detail – of the killing
of the battle-weary Sisera by Jael, the Kenite woman. Judges 5 is the poetic version
of Deborah's triumph.

Gideon

In Judges 6–8 we find a collection of stories about Gideon from a number of different
traditions. The stories seek to establish that Yahweh is God, and not Baal; that
Yahweh is ruler, and not any earthly monarch.

Gideon's first task was to destroy his father's altar to Baal; his second, to set about
tackling the problem of the Midianites, one of Israel's most troublesome enemies at
the time. Gideon declined the offer of the kingship of Israel, but one of his sons –
Abimelech – claimed to have inherited the right to kingship. He 'reigned' briefly
over Shechem but in no sense was he a king of Israel. After Gideon had overcome
the Midianites, Israel 'had rest for forty years in the days of Gideon' (Judges 8.28).

Tola

From the tribe of Issachar, and the son of Puah. He 'lived at Shamir in the hill
country of Ephraim and rose to deliver Israel' (Judges 10.1). We are not told from
what or from whom Tola delivered Israel. We are told that he was judge in Israel for
twenty-three years.

Jair

A Gileadite and a wealthy man, who judged Israel for twenty-two years. About his
exploits we know nothing (Judges 10.3–5).

Jephthah

A successful general responsible for resisting the Ammonite occupation of Gilead.
Subsequently, he served as a judge of Israel (Judges 10.6–12.7). Some of the stories

in the accounts of Jephthah are confused threads of a number of ancient traditions including the self-sacrifice of his daughter and a battle with Ephraimites. Jephthah judged Israel for six years and was buried in Gilead.

Ibzan

Mentioned as a successor to Jephthah, who was judge for seven years. His claim to fame appears to be that his thirty sons and thirty daughters all married outside his clan (Judges 12.8–10).

Elon

Judged Israel for ten years. He was a Zebulunite and was buried in Aijalon (Judges 12.11).

Abdon

Judged for eight years. He was the son of Hillel, and a reasonably wealthy man. He was buried in the land of Ephraim (Judges 12.13–15).

Samson

The large cycle of folk-hero stories about the exploits of Samson against the Philistines are collected together in Judges 13–16. In fact, he was in his time clearly more of a local hero than a national figure, though he was renowned for being a successful thorn in the side of the Philistines. He is considered to be the last judge of Israel.

Eli

The record of Eli's death declares that he was a judge who had judged Israel for forty years (1 Samuel 4.18).
(see *Priests and High Priests – Eli*)

Samuel

Although in many respects Samuel fulfilled the role of judge, he was much more than that. He was the figure who was centre stage throughout the transition between the Israel of the judges and the Israel of the monarchy.

Samuel became the servant of Eli, the priest. By means of a series of midnight voices, Eli realized that God would appoint Samuel as his successor at Shiloh. This occurred when the Philistines removed the Ark of the Covenant from Shiloh and defeated the Israelites in a number of battles. The Philistines fortunes were reversed by Samuel's successes and by the terrible afflictions they suffered when the Ark was taken into their territory. Under Samuel, captured towns were recovered and the Philistines returned the Ark. It remained for twenty years at Kiriath-jearim until David installed it in his new capital at Jerusalem.

In response to the murmurings of the people Samuel gave them Saul as king but, due to Saul's shortcomings, God caused Samuel to anoint David, the youngest son of Jesse (1 Samuel 1–6).

Kenites

Among the inhabitants of the lands promised to Abram (later, Abraham) on the day 'the Lord made a covenant with Abram' (Genesis 15.18–21). They were nomads of the desert region in the south of Canaan and ultimately settled alongside the Amalekites in 'the wilderness of Judah, which lies in the Negeb, near Arad' (Judges 1.16). The Kenites were reliable allies of Israel from the days of the Exodus – Moses' father-in-law, Hobab, was a Kenite (Judges 4.11) – and continued to be so thereafter. It is thought that they were skilled in copper smelting. Certainly there is evidence of copper mining in this area of the Negeb.

Diagram
Map of Canaan (6)

Kenizzites

The Kenizzites, along with the Kenites, were among the inhabitants of the lands promised to Abram (later, Abraham) (Genesis 15.18–21). They moved farther south, eventually, and were assimilated into the tribe of Judah. However, Kenaz, the son of Esau and great grandson of Abraham, was considered to be the father of the Edomite clan of the Kenizzites. (Esau was the ancestor of the Edomites and Amalekites.)

Diagrams
Family of Abraham (2)
Map of Canaan (6)

Kings of the United Kingdom of Israel

Saul

The son of Kish the Benjaminite, anointed as first king of a united Israel, following the two-hundred years or so of the period of the judges of Israel, after he had defeated Nahash, the king of Ammonites. When Saul failed to press home his advantage over the Amalekites and kill King Agag, Samuel, under divine guidance, took the responsibility for despatching Agag. He caused Agag to be brought before him and 'hewed Agag in pieces before the Lord in Gilgal' (1 Samuel 15.32, 33).

Samuel, depressed by Saul's general ineptitude, anointed David, the youngest son of Jesse, to be king in his place. The remainder of Saul's reign is the story of the growing disenchantment with Saul and the rise of David.
(see *Ancestors of King Saul*)

Ishbaal (Ish-bosheth)

The son of Saul; in him, those who opposed the kingship of David, saw the successor to Saul. Abner, 'commander of Saul's army . . . brought him [Ishbaal] over to Mahanaim. He made him king over Gilead . . . and over all Israel. Ishbaal . . . reigned for two years' (2 Samuel 2.8–11).

David

David became harpist in the king's court in order to alleviate Saul's depression. David rose in prominence in the court and achieved renown with the killing of Goliath and his prowess in battle. Inevitably, the declining king began to feel vulnerable, and a love-hate relationship with David ensued and cloaked the remaining years of Saul's reign (1 Samuel 16–31).

· After the death of Saul, David settled in Hebron and was anointed 'king over the house of Judah' (2 Samuel 2.1–4). 'The time that David was king in Hebron over the house of Judah was seven years and six months' (2 Samuel 2.11). At the end of this term, Ishbaal's general, Abner, defected to David and made peace with him but Joab, the general of David's army, was incensed and had Abner killed. When Ishbaal was assassinated, David was anointed king over all Israel. His capital was moved to Jerusalem after he took it from the control of the Jebusites. 'At Jerusalem he reigned over Israel and Judah for thirty-three years' (2 Samuel 5.5). David reigned, probably, from 1000–993 BC as King of Judah, and from 993–961 BC as king over a united Israel.

(see *Ancestors of King David*)

Solomon

Having despatched the supporters of his elder brother, Adonijah, Solomon succeeded to his father's throne. He reigned until about 922 BC. Although discontent was then beginning to show itself – Solomon had to contend with the rebellion of Jeroboam – and old enemies of Israel still lurked in the background waiting their moment, Solomon's reign was notable for peace within the borders of Israel. He had consolidated David's territorial gains and expanded the kingdom. He was famous throughout the region for the grandeur and sumptuousness of his court. However, he had introduced into his court influences of pagan religions (1 Kings 11.1–13).

Rehoboam

The son of Solomon, Rehoboam, succeeded for a short time in the year of Solomon's death, and before the kingdom divided. The northern tribes became the kingdom of Israel under Jeroboam; the kingdom of Judah, under Rehoboam, comprised the tribes of Judah and Benjamin (1 Kings 12).

Kings of the Kingdom of Israel

At the division of the kingdom, Jeroboam became king of the northern kingdom of Israel. Israel survived for two hundred years until the fall of Samaria – the northern kingdom's capital – at the hands of the Assyrians in about 722 BC.

Jeroboam

When a servant in the court of Solomon, Jeroboam conspired against the king and was subsequently forced to flee to Egypt. He returned after the death of Solomon and was made king over the northern tribes after Rehoboam had alienated them by indicating that he would treat them no less harshly than his father treated them.

Jeroboam created a capital for himself at Shechem and principal places of worship at Dan and at Bethel. But for those two ostensibly holy places he made two golden calves for the worship of the people. 'The time that Jeroboam reigned was twenty-two years; then he slept with his ancestors, and his son Nadab succeeded him' (1 Kings 14.20).

Nadab

He reigned for only two years and was struck down by his successor Baasha while Israel was laying siege to the Philistine city of Gibbethon (1 Kings 15.27, 28).

Baasha

He killed all the house of Jeroboam in order to protect his precarious position. Although he reigned for about thirteen years, the prophet Jehu predicted his downfall because of his return to the ways of Jeroboam (1 Kings 16.1–7).

Elah

The son of Baasha and was on the throne just two years. His servant Zimri conspired against Elah and killed him and all his relations, and then reigned in his place (1 Kings 16.8–14).

Zimri

When the Israelite army heard that Zimri had usurped the king, they made the commander of the army, Omri, king, and they besieged Tirzah where Zimri was staying. Zimri saw that all was lost and burned the house around him and died. 'Zimri reigned for seven days in Tirzah' (1 Kings 16.15).

Tibni and Omri

'Then were the people of Israel divided into two parts; half of the people followed Tibni son of Ginath, to make him king, and half followed Omri' (1 Kings 16.21). Tibni was overpowered by Omri's followers and killed.

Omri

He reigned for six years at Tirzah. Then he built the city of Samaria and made his capital there. He reigned for a further six years (1 Kings 16.24).

Ahab

In terms of years, Ahab's reign was relatively successful. He was the son of Omri, and he was on the throne for twenty-two years. However, he married Jezebel, a daughter of the Phoenician king, and caused Israel to worship Baal. This set the stage for Elijah the prophet and the story of the massacre of the pagan priests.

Ahab and Jehoshaphat of Judah entered a joint campaign against Aram. Ahab, disguised as a soldier, was shot with an arrow and died from his wounds (1 Kings 16.29–22.50).

Ahaziah

Ahab's son who reigned for two years. The injury he sustained when he fell from a window brought him into contact with Elijah. He took to his bed and died from the injury (2 Kings 1).

Jehoram (Joram)

Confusingly, this son of Ahab, who succeeded his brother Ahaziah, was on the throne of Israel about the same time that Jehoram, son of Jehoshaphat, was on the throne of Judah. Before that occurred, Jehoram entered into an alliance with Jehoshaphat to put down the rebellion of the king of Moab. The alliance was repulsed. Later, Jehoram was injured in a campaign against the Arameans but recovered. However, Jehu, son of Jehoshaphat (not, incidentally, the king of Judah) having been anointed king by Elisha, conspired to kill Jehoram and succeeded in ambushing and killing both Jehoram and Ahaziah of Judah (2 Kings 3–9).

Kings of the Kingdom of Israel

Jehu
Succeeded Jehoram and set about the removal of all descendants of the house of Ahab. This was a difficult period in Israel's history. We know from external evidence that tribute was paid to Shalmaneser III of Assyria in the year 842 BC. Furthermore, 'in those days the Lord began to trim off parts of Israel. Hazael [king of Aram (Syria)] defeated them throughout the territory of Israel' (2 Kings 10.32). Jehu was succeeded by his son, Jehoahaz. Jehu had reigned for twenty-eight years.

Jehoahaz
Jehoahaz reigned for seventeen years. His battles against the Arameans were costly in terms of the depletion of his armed forces. His son, Joash, succeeded him (2 Kings 13.1–9).

Joash (Jehoash)
Again, there is a short period when both Israel and Judah have kings of the same name. He reigned for seventeen years and enjoyed some success over the Arameans in that he was able to recover some of the towns of Israel from the hands of King Ben-hadad, the son of Hazael (2 Kings 13.10).

Jeroboam II
The son of Joash, he reigned for just over forty years. His dates are, probably, 786 BC to 746 BC. During his reign he recovered more of the lands lost to the Arameans (2 Kings 14.23–29).

Zechariah
The son of Jeroboam II and reigned for only six months. 'Shallum son of Jabesh conspired against him, and struck him down in public and killed him, and reigned in place of him' (2 Kings 15.10).

Shallum
Shallum was only one month into his reign when 'Menahem son of Gadi . . . struck down Shallum son of Jabesh in Samaria and killed him' (2 Kings 15.14).

Menahem
His reign lasted ten years but it was an uncomfortable period for the kingdom of Israel. Assyria, once again beginning to flex its muscles, invaded under Tiglath-pileser III (named, Pul, in the Old Testament) and exacted large sums in tribute from Israel (2 Kings 15.17–22).

Pekahiah
Menahem's son, who reigned for two years. His captain, Pekah, conspired against him and, with a small force of Gileadites, killed him in Samaria and took the throne (2 Kings 15.23–26).

Pekah
He reigned for twenty years but much land was lost to Assyria during this time. He died at the hand of Hoshea, his successor (2 Kings 15.27–31).

Hoshea

He reigned for nine years. During this time, tribute was paid to Assyria in vast quantities. Hoshea attempted an alliance against Assyria with Egypt, but his plan was discovered and he was imprisoned in the Assyrian court. By 722 BC Samaria had fallen and many Israelites transported to Assyria and the lands of Israel filled with people from Mesopotamian cities and towns (2 Kings 17).

Kings of the Kingdom of Judah

At the division of the kingdom, Rehoboam became the king of the southern kingdom of Judah. Judah survived until the fall of Jerusalem at the hand of Babylon on 587 BC. (Biblical references to 1 and 2 Kings are given but the reader should also consult the parallel histories contained in 2 Chronicles.)

Rehoboam

The son of Solomon, he reigned for seventeen years in Jerusalem. During his reign, Shishak (Sheshonk) of Egypt sacked Jerusalem and removed the gold plate. Egypt largely had control over Palestine at this time (1 Kings 14.21–31).

Abijam

The son of Rehoboam, he reigned for three years. He continued the wars with Israel that had begun in his father's day. He was succeeded by his son, Asa (1 Kings 15.1–8).

Asa

A successful king in terms of the length of his reign and in the eyes of the writers of 1 Kings 15.9–15. He took steps to remove the corruption of the temple worship established from time to time since the days of David. During his reign he entered into an alliance with Ben-hadad I of Aram against the northern kingdom of Israel. Asa's son Jehoshaphat succeeded.

Jehoshaphat

He reigned for twenty-five years in Jerusalem. 'He walked in all the way of his father Asa; he did not turn aside from it, doing what was right in the sight of the Lord' (1 Kings 22.43). 'Jehoshaphat also made peace with the king of Israel' (1 Kings 22.44). Jehoshaphat's son Jehoram succeeded.

Jehoram (Joram)

He reigned for eight years. He was tainted with the sin of the house of Israel's King Ahab, as he had married Athaliah, Ahab's daughter. Jehoram attacked Edom in the south when they 'set up a king of their own' (2 Kings 8.21).

Ahaziah

The son of Jehoram of Judah. He reigned for one year only. He entered into an alliance with Israel against Aram.

Entrapped by Jehu, both Ahaziah and Jehoram of Israel were killed (2 Kings 9.27–29).

Kings of the Kingdom of Judah

Athaliah

The daughter of King Ahab of Israel, she was Ahaziah's mother and, on the death of her son, sought to exterminate the rest of the family but Ahaziah's sister hid his son, Joash (Jehoash) and 'he remained with her for six years, hidden in the house of the Lord while Athaliah reigned over the land' (2 Kings 11.1–3). After six years, the priest Jehoiada had Joash proclaimed king and anointed. The captains of the guard were instructed to put Athaliah to death with the sword.

Joash (Jehoash)

He reigned prudently, though not spectacularly, for forty years. When Jerusalem was threatened by Hazael of Aram, Joash gave him the valuables from the treasury, and Hazael withdrew. 'His servants [Joash's] arose, made a conspiracy and killed Joash in the house of Millo, on the way that goes down to Silla' (2 Kings 12.19–21).

Amaziah

The son of Joash of Judah, he reigned for twenty-nine years. He enjoyed success against the Edomites but failed in a battle with Israel and was taken hostage by Joash of Israel. The king of Israel marched him to Jerusalem and took all the valuables of the treasury, and returned with them to Samaria. Fifteen years later, Amaziah was assassinated and his son Azariah put on the throne (2 Kings 14.1–22).

Azariah (Uzziah)

Azariah of 2 Kings 15 is the Uzziah of 2 Kings 15.32 and Isaiah 1. He reigned for fifty-two years in Jerusalem and, in the earlier part of his reign made significant successes, particularly against Edom and the Philistine cites that threatened Judah's borders. He dithered over whether or not he should join an alliance against Assyria, and in the end did not.

Jotham

Azariah's son, he reigned over Judah for sixteen years. He was succeeded by his son, Ahaz.

Ahaz

As his father had done, he reigned over Judah for sixteen years. He successfully withstood a joint attack from Aram and Israel but lost territory to Edom in the south. In exchange for protection against Aram and Israel, Ahaz paid handsome sums to the Assyrian kings (2 Kings 16).

Hezekiah

The son of Ahaz, he inherited nothing more than a country under the heel of Assyria. He paid huge sums to King Sennacherib of Assyria. However, when encamped about Jerusalem, Sennacherib could not take the city and, in answer to Hezekiah's prayer, the Assyrian army was devastated by the death of around one hundred and eighty-five thousand soldiers in one night. Isaiah predicted that the fate of the house of Judah would come from Babylon (2 Kings 18–20).

Manasseh

The assertion that Manasseh reigned for fifty-five years is now taken as something of an exaggeration by about ten years. Manasseh restored pagan worship to the temple and 'he rebuilt the high places that his father Hezekiah had destroyed; he erected altars for Baal, made a sacred pole, as King Ahab of Israel had done' (2 Kings 21.3). His son Amon succeeded him.

Amon
He was killed by his servants after only two years on the throne and was succeeded by Josiah his son (2 Kings 21.19–26).

Josiah
He reigned for thirty-one years in Jerusalem and it was during his reign that the core of the Book of Deuteronomy was found in the temple. It was this book of the law upon which the new Israel was founded after the return of the Judean captives from exile in Babylon. Judah was now in a parlous state positioned as it was between two greater powers, those of Assyria in the north and Egypt in the south. Following Josiah's death in battle with Egypt, Judah became nothing more than an adjunct to Egypt (2 Kings 22–23).

Jehoahaz
The son of Josiah, he reigned only three months in Jerusalem. Pharaoh Neco removed Jehoahaz to Egypt and placed Eliakim, another son of Josiah, on the throne (2 Kings 23.31–35).

Jehoiakim (Eliakim)
Pharaoh Neco changed Eliakim's name to Jehoiakim. Jehoiakim reigned for eleven years in Jerusalem (2 Kings 23.36, 37). By this time, Babylon was the most powerful force in the region and Jehoiakim was obliged to pay tribute to King Nebuchadnezzar (more correctly, Nebuchadrezzar). (The Babylonian king's father had defeated Egypt in the battle of Carchemish in 605 BC.)

Jehoiachin
The son of Jehoiakim, he reigned for three months and surrendered to Nebuchadnezzar when he besieged Jerusalem. The royal family and many other captives were taken to Babylon. Nebuchadnezzar left the poorest people in Jerusalem and made Jehoiachin's uncle, Mattaniah, king in his place, but changed his name to Zedekiah (2 Kings 24.8–12). Jehoiachin lived for many years in exile in Babylon.
(In the book of Esther, he is named Jeconiah.)

Zedekiah (Mattaniah)
He reigned for eleven years in Jerusalem but towards the end of his reign he rebelled against Babylon, and Jerusalem was ultimately ransacked. Many others were now taken into exile. Zedekiah himself was blinded after watching the slaughter of his sons before he too was taken to Babylon. Nebuchadnezzar appointed Gedaliah as governor over the people who remained in the land of Judah (2 Kings 24.13–20; 2 Kings 25).

Diagram
Broad Parallel Histories (16–22)

Kings of Other Lands

Many foreign kings played important roles in the fortunes and misfortunes of the Hebrews and the Children of Israel. It is worth noting a few of them.

Abimelech
The king of Gerar, a city in the land later occupied by the Philistines. On entering the land of Abimelech, Abraham pretended that Sarah was his sister, rather than his wife. Precisely the same story appears later but with Isaac in place of Abraham (Genesis 20, 21 and 26).

Achish
The king of Gath. David fostered good relations with him when fleeing from Saul (1 Samuel 21.10–15 and 28, 29).

Adoni-bezek
Judah and Simeon defeated an army of Canaanites and Perizzites at Bezek; they caught King Adoni-bezek and cut off his thumbs and big toes (Judges 1.1–7).

Adoni-zedek
The king of Jerusalem who, together with four other kings brought together an army against Joshua. After the battle, the five kings were hanged (Joshua 10.1–27).

Agag
King Agag's life was spared after Saul had defeated the Amalekites. Through Samuel, God showed his displeasure with Saul (1 Samuel 15.7–33).

Ahasuerus
Usually identified with King Xerxes, the fifth king of Persia (486–465 BC). He made Esther queen in place of the disgraced Vashti (Esther 2.15–18).
(see *Persians*)

Ahmose
The pharaoh (*c.*1570–1550 BC) responsible for the expulsion of the Hyksos from Egypt. It may be that Ahmose was the new king who 'arose over Egypt, who did not know Joseph' (Exodus 1.8), though some scholars still favour Seti I and, therefore, a date far closer to the Exodus.

Amraphel
King of Shinar and one of a confederacy of four minor clan leaders who waged war with kingdoms around the Dead Sea (Genesis 14.1–16).

Artaxerxes I
He was the son of Xerxes (Ahasuerus) and third king of the Persian Empire (Esther 11.2 – contained in the Apocrypha of some versions of the Bible).

Arioch
Arioch of Ellasar joined Amraphel in the wars against the cities around the Dead Sea (Genesis 14.1).

Ashur-banipal

King of Assyria and son of King Esarhaddon and flourished from 668–626 BC. He may be the Osnappar of Ezra 4.10.

Balak

The king of Moab who engaged the help of Balaam to place a curse upon the Israelites after seeing what had happened to King Og of Bashan and King Sihon of the Amorites (Numbers 22).

Belshazzar

Not the king of Babylon but the regent of his father, Nabonidus. (Nabonidus preferred to live in an oasis outside Babylon.) It was Belshazzar who surrendered Babylon to Gobyras, a general of Cyrus the Great, in 539 BC (Daniel 5, 7, 8 – however, the Book of Daniel is not, of course, an accurate history of the Babylonian rulers).

Ben-hadad I

This was the king of Aram (Syria) who, in an alliance with King Asa of Judah attacked Israel (1 Kings 15.16–24).

Ben-hadad II

The second Ben-hadad was the son of King Hazael of Aram but no relation to the first. Hazael had killed Ben-hadad I and taken the throne (2 Kings 13.1–9).

Candace

Candace was the title rather than a personal name of the queens of Meroe, in Nubia. We are acquainted with one such as the owner of the eunuch converted by Philip the deacon (Acts 8.26–39).

Chedorlaomer

King of Elam and one of the four kings who, with King Amraphel, waged war with the kingdoms around the Dead Sea (Genesis 14.1–16).

Cyrus the Great

The first emperor of the Persian Empire, which lasted from about 550 BC until conquered by Alexander the Great.

Cyrus rose from kingship of an Elamite province of the empire of the Medes, but rebelled and in 559 BC defeated the king of the Medes. He declared himself to be the king of the Persians and set about securing the whole of the Median Empire. He then defeated Croesus of Lydia and accepted the surrender of Belshazzar, who was regent for his father Nabonidus, in 539 BC. After Cyrus had added Babylon to his conquests, he permitted the return of those taken captive from Jerusalem (2 Chronicles 36.22, 23).

Darius I

King of Persia from 522 to 468 BC. He was responsible for executing Cyrus's decree concerning the rebuilding of the temple at Jerusalem (Ezra 6.1–18).

Kings of Other Lands

Debir
King of Eglon and one of the five kings who unsuccessfully opposed Joshua (Joshua 10.1–27).

Eglon
The head of a successful coalition comprising the Moabites, the Amalekites and the Ammonites. This coalition defeated the Israelites and Eglon exacted tribute from them for eighteen years. King Eglon was eventually murdered by Ehud, the first judge of Israel (Judges 3.12–30).

Esarhaddon
The son of Sennacherib of Assyria. He ruled over Assyria and, after rebuilding Babylon, which was destroyed by his father, over Babylon as well (2 Kings 19.35–37).

Esther
She replaced Vashti as Ahasuerus' (Xerxes') queen. (Esther)

Ethbaal
The father of Jezebel, the wife of King Ahab of Israel. He was king of the Sidonians, who were the Phoenicians who lived in and around Sidon (1 Kings 16.31).

Evil-merodach (more correctly, Amel-marduk)
The successor to his father, Nebuchadnezzar in 562 BC. According to 2 Kings 25.27–30, it was he who released King Jehoiachin of Judah from prison in Babylon. 'So Jehoiachin put aside his prison clothes. Every day of his life he dined regularly in the king's presence.'

Hadadezer
King of Zobah who led the Arameans against David and was defeated (1 Chronicles 18.3–8).

Hanun
In order to establish himself as a force to be reckoned with, King Hanun of the Ammonites had the temerity to humiliate King David's emissaries by having half their beards shaved (2 Samuel 10. 1–5).

Hiram
King of Tyre who was a close friend of David and Solomon to whom he supplied cedar for the construction of the temple (1 Kings·5.1–6).

Hoham
King of Hebron and one of the five kings who unsuccessfully opposed Joshua and the Gibeonites (Joshua 10.1–27).

Horam
King of Gezer who came to the assistance of Lachish after Joshua had annihilated the population. 'Joshua struck him and his people, leaving no survivors' (Joshua 10.31–33).

Jabin
King of Hazor who assembled a large force with the help of other kings of the northern part of Canaan in order to oppose the Israelites. Joshua defeated them all and took their towns (Joshua 11.1–15).

Japhia
King of Lachish and one of the five kings who unsuccessfully opposed Joshua and the Gibeonites (Joshua 10.1–27).

Jobab
One of the kings of Edom before Jacob's family settled in Canaan (Genesis 36.31–34).

Jobab
King of Madon and part of the force assembled by King Jabin of Hazor (Joshua 11.1–15).

Merodach-baladan
The usurper-king of Babylon, and son of Baladan. He twice became king of Babylon and twice reverted to a mere Chaldean sheikh. After the death of Sargon II, Merodach-baladan tried to interest King Hezekiah of Judah in supporting his stance against Assyrian rule. Merodach-baladan was deposed as king of Babylon when Sennacherib came to the throne of Assyria (2 Kings 20.12-19).

Mesha
King of Moab who paid tribute to King Ahab of Israel. Mesha rebelled against his successor, Jehoram, and a battle between the Moabites and an alliance of Israel, Judah and Edom ensued. The outcome was inconclusive (2 Kings 3.4–27).

Nabonidus
The successor to King Evil-merodach of Babylon. He preferred to live outside Babylon and leave the running of the empire to his son, Belshazzar, as regent.

Nabopolassar
The father of Nebuchadnezzar and the Babylonian king who finally freed Babylon from Assyrian domination. He reigned from 626 BC to 605 BC.

Nahash
Nahash was the king of Ammon defeated by Saul at Jabesh-gilead (1 Samuel 11.1–11).

Nebuchadnezzar (more correctly, Nebuchadrezzar)
The successor to the throne of Babylon after his father Nabopolassar. After the defeat of Egypt at the hands of the armies of Babylon, Nebuchadnezzar turned his full attention on Jerusalem and first took King Jehoiachim and most of the royal family to Babylon in 597 BC (2 Kings 24.6–12). The second deportation, and the more significant in terms of numbers, occurred ten years later.

Kings of Other Lands

Neco
The second king of the twenty-sixth Egyptian dynasty. He reigned from 609 BC to 594 BC. King Josiah of Judah was killed in battle with the Egyptians at Megiddo and Judah was made subject to Egypt. However, Nabopolassar sent his son, Nebuchadnezzar against Neco at Carchemish in 605 BC, and Egypt was soundly defeated (2 Kings 23.28–35).

Og
The king of Bashan who was defeated by the Israelites after they had defeated and taken the lands of Sihon, king of the Amorites (Numbers 21.33–35).

Piram
The king of Jarmuth who unsuccessfully opposed Joshua and the Gibeonites (Joshua 10.1–27).

Pul
In 2 Kings 15, Tiglath-pileser III is referred to also as Pul. (In the Babylonian lists of kings, he is named Pulu.)
(see *Tiglath-pileser III*)

Rameses II
Pharaoh of Egypt and the son of Seti I. He reigned from 1290 BC to 1224 BC and was probably the pharaoh of the Exodus, though some scholars have made arguments against this proposition.

Rezin
The king of Aram who besieged Jerusalem in the days of King Ahaz of Judah. Ahaz sought aid from the Assyrian king, Tiglath-pileser III (2 Kings 16.5–7).

Sargon II
King of Assyria from about 721 BC to 705 BC. He may have been the son of Tiglath-pileser III and brother to the murdered Shalmaneser V, whom he succeeded. He was, perhaps, responsible for the final defeat of Samaria and the deportation of its citizens. Sargon II expelled Merodach-baladan from the throne of Babylon and then ruled both Assyria and Babylon (2 Kings 17.5, 6).

Sennacherib
He succeeded Sargon II and reigned from 704 BC to 681 BC. Sennacherib was responsible for capturing the fortified cities of Judah and exacting large sums from Hezekiah, king of Judah (2 Kings 18.13–16).

Seti I
Pharaoh from 1305 BC to 1290 BC and was probably the pharaoh during whose reign the Exodus was conceived, planned and, may be, executed, though it is likely that the Exodus took place at the beginning of the reign of Seti's son, Rameses II. Some scholars will argue that Seti I may have been the pharaoh 'who did not know Joseph' (Exodus 1.8) and enslaved the Hebrews, but the stronger argument places the enslavement much earlier, during the reign of Ahmose, some two hundred years earlier.

Shalmaneser III
Although it is ignored in the books of the Old Testament, King Jehu of Israel paid tribute to Shalmaneser III of Assyria around 840 BC in order to protect Israel from the Arameans (Syrians).

Shalmaneser V
He succeeded his father Tiglath-pileser III, was murdered shortly before the capitulation of Samaria, and was succeeded by Sargon II. It was he who imprisoned King Hoshea of Israel and began the final siege of Samaria (2 Kings 17.1–4).

Sheba
This was the Queen *of* Sheba rather than the name of the queen. There is no agreement as to the precise whereabouts of Sheba from which its queen visited King Solomon. But the story illustrates that Solomon was always intent upon making contact and trade with countries well beyond his boundaries (1 Kings 10.1–13).

Shishak (Sheshonk)
He re-established Egyptian might with the founding of the XXII dynasty. He attacked Jerusalem shortly after the death of Solomon (1 Kings 14.25–28).

Sihon
King of the Amorites who was attacked and defeated by the Israelites after refusing them safe passage through his lands (Numbers 21.21–35).

Tiglath-pileser III
The Assyrian king responsible for re-establishing Assyria's dominance over Mesopotamia and elsewhere. His reign began in about 745 BC. In the reign of King Pekah of Israel, Tiglath-pileser captured parts of northern Israel and took many into captivity. In the meantime, King Ahaz of Judah curried favour with Tiglath-pileser and lavished presents upon him in exchange for help in his battle against King Rezin of Aram (2 Kings 15.29 and 16.5–7).
(see *Pul*)

Tou
The king of Hamath who sent word to David after hearing of his success against Hadadezer. 'He sent his son Hadoram to King David to greet him and to congratulate him, because he had fought Hadadezer and defeated him. Now Hadadezer had often been at war with Tou' (1 Chronicles 18.9–11).

Diagram
Broad Parallel Histories (16–22)

Korahites

The descendants of Korah and a body responsible for service as gatekeepers and as psalmists and singers from the time of worship in the wilderness to the temple worship of King David's day, and of the post-exilic period (1 Chronicles 26.19). (Korah, Dathan and Abiram were responsible for the rebellion against the Moses and Aaron in the wilderness (Numbers 26.9–11).)
(see *Aaronites*)

Letter Writers of the New Testament

Diagram
Tree of the Tribe of Levi (4)

Letter Writers of the New Testament

There are twenty-one letters (epistles) in the New Testament. They were written for the edification and instruction of the many growing components of the Early Church in Palestine and around the Mediterranean coasts. They cannot all, however, be attributed to the writers traditionally associated with them. The use of the name of a well-known and respected leader of the Early Church gave a piece of writing authority it might not otherwise have enjoyed. Pseudepigraphy was, therefore, not uncommon, and was, for the most part, intended to point the reader or listener in the direction of the teaching of the person so named. Scholars disagree about many of the letter writers and dates of the letters. The following details reflect what finds widest acceptance in the world of biblical scholarship.

The Letter to the Romans
Paul wrote this letter to the Christians in Rome shortly before he visited Jerusalem. He may have written the letter in Corinth in about AD 57.

The First Letter to the Corinthians
Paul and Sosthenes wrote this letter to the Church in Corinth. Sosthenes probably played a subordinate role in the writing. The letter, written in Ephesus, dates from about AD 52.

The Second Letter to the Corinthians
This is probably a compound of a number of letters, written in AD 55 or AD 56 by Paul while he was in Macedonia.

The Letter to the Galatians
Paul was probably in Ephesus when he wrote this letter to be passed around the young churches in Galatia. It dates from AD 53 or AD 54.

The Letter to the Ephesians
It is likely that this general letter dates from the 70s. When it was first known, it was not addressed specifically to the Ephesians. The style of writing is not typically that of Paul, and scholars no longer attribute the letter to him.

The Letter to the Philippians
This was a personal letter to the Christians in Philippi – a city inhabited by Greeks, Macedonians and Romans – written by Paul in about AD 55 while he was in prison in Ephesus.

The Letter to the Colossians
There is not general agreement about the authorship of this letter. In places it alludes to a number of Paul's letters, and even makes mention of the man, Onesimus, among others (Colossians 4.9). If Paul was the writer, the letter was probably written while in prison at Ephesus in about AD 54. It may be that Paul merely added the greetings at the conclusion of the letter to something he did not dictate. The letter is addressed to Christians in Colossae, whose ruins are apparent today in modern Turkey.

The First Letter to the Thessalonians

This letter is likely to be the earliest extant Christian text, with the possible exception of the Letter of James, written as it was in about AD 50 by Paul while he was in Corinth. It was probably composed shortly after Paul's first visit to Thessalonica and may have been a reply to a letter received by Paul.

The Second Letter to the Thessalonians

This letter seems to follow the first rather slavishly. It was, probably, written by a follower of Paul.

The First and Second Letters to Timothy and the Letter to Titus

The three Pastoral Epistles, as they are often called, were written by someone who desired to show the importance of Paul's teaching as preached by people of the calibre of Timothy and Titus.

Personal details contained within these letters suggest an author other than Paul, even though they attempt to do the opposite. Indeed, it is not thought that Paul would have written a personal letter to his companions in this way. Furthermore, the list of attributes of a candidate for the diaconate or the episcopate, contained in the third chapter of the first letter to Timothy, places the trilogy late in the first century.

The Letter to Philemon

Paul wrote the letter to Philemon from prison in Ephesus. It was a personal letter to Philemon about the slave, Onesimus, who had been serving Paul in prison. The letter dates from about AD 55.

The Letter to the Hebrews

This letter, by an unknown hand, was written early in the second half of the first century to a Christian community somewhere in Italy. The title *to the Hebrews* was added long after the letter was first known.

The Letter of James

This letter may well have been written by James the 'brother' of Jesus, and first bishop of Jerusalem – and there is no real evidence to suggest otherwise – to the Greek-speaking Jewish Christians. If so, it is likely to date from the early AD 40s, and so rival the first letter to the Thessalonians as the earliest extant piece of Christian writing. However, many scholars date the letter after AD 70 and assert that, as the attribution is much later than the letter, doubt is cast upon the true identity of the author.

(see *Brothers of Jesus*)

The First Letter of Peter

This letter is a general epistle to Christians written in the second half of the first century by the followers of Peter after his martyrdom there between AD 64 and AD 66 during the time of the Emperor Nero. The letter is written in finely polished Greek.

The Second Letter of Peter

This is another general letter to Christians, possibly earlier than the first letter of Peter, which stresses the importance of Peter and his teaching. The writer was certainly not the writer of the first letter of Peter.

The Three Letters of John

The first letter is a carefully written document, which may well come from the hand of the writer of the Gospel of John; the second letter does contain suggestions of the first; the third and the second admit of common authorship in the person of John the Elder. The most satisfactory conclusion is that the Gospel and all three letters arise out of the same *school* – that of the Apostle John and his followers. The letters are likely to be of a date later than AD 90, the date of the Gospel.
(see *Evangelists*)

The Letter of Jude

Most scholars agree that this letter dates from before AD 70. There is not by any means unanimous support for the proposition that Jude, the brother of James, the first bishop of Jerusalem, wrote this letter. However, there is no substantial evidence to the contrary. The letter suggests that the second letter of Peter relied heavily on the letter of Jude indicating that, in the Early Church, this letter was held in high esteem.
(see *Brothers of Jesus*)

Levi, Tribe of

Levi was the third son of Jacob and the third by Leah. 'Again she conceived and bore a son and said, "Now this time will my husband be joined to me because I have borne him three sons"; therefore he was named Levi' (Genesis 29.34). He was the ancestor of the tribe of Levi. The Levites had no tribal territory but were, when the time came, dedicated to the service of Aaron, and to the priesthood (Joshua 13.33). However, they were allotted forty-eight towns together with pastureland throughout Israel (Joshua 21.41).

Diagrams
Children of Israel (3)
Tree of the Tribe of Levi (4)

Maacathites

The Maacathites were among the inhabitants of the land of Canaan encountered by the Israelites. They inhabited the land below Mount Hermon, on the east of the Jordan, and above the land of the Geshurites. The Geshurites lived on the eastern side of the Sea of Galilee (Joshua 12.5). 'Yet the Israelites did not drive out the Geshurites or the Maacathites but Geshur and Maacath live within Israel to this day' (Joshua 13.13).
(see *Canaanites, Geshurites*)

Diagram
Map of Canaan (6)

Maccabees

The revolt by Mattathias against the Seleucid king, Antiochus IV, who had begun to introduce and encourage pagan religious practices in Judea, ultimately resulted in his son, Judas Maccabeus, becoming the ruler of Jerusalem in 164 BC (1 Maccabees 2.15–28). Judas was succeeded by his brothers Jonathan and Simon. Mattathias's

grandson, John Hyrcanus, assumed the title of king, and ruled from 134 BC to 104 BC. His son, Aristobulus, succeeded and began to enforce conversion to Judaism in a brutal and savage way. Aristobulus's brother, Alexander, succeeded in the same year (104 BC) and remained on the throne until 76 BC. Internal strife precipitated the decline of the Maccabees and brought the dynasty to an end. Coincidentally, the Roman general, Pompey, was extending the influence of the Roman Empire east-wards and placed Hyrcanus, the priestly brother of the last king, Aristobulus II, in control under the thumb of Rome, in 63 BC (1 and 2 Maccabees).
(see Greeks, Hasmoneans, Herods)

Manasseh, Tribe of

Manasseh was the first-born son of Joseph. Both sons – Manasseh and Ephraim – were adopted by Jacob and became tribal ancestors along with their uncles. The blessing of Joseph's sons by Jacob, and his preference for Ephraim over the first-born, Manasseh (Genesis 48.13–20) perhaps contains echoes of Jacob's deception of Isaac, when he was preferred over his brother Esau, the firstborn (Genesis 27.18–29). The Josephite tribe of Manasseh was allocated land either side of the Jordan – on the western side, between the tribal land of Issachar to the north and Ephraim to the south, and, on the eastern side, between the tribal land of Gad and the land of Bashan (Joshua 13.29–31 and Joshua 17.1–12).

Diagrams
Children of Israel (3)
Tribal Lands of Israel (8)

Maonites

Referred to, along with Amalekites and Sidonians, as enemies of Israel (Judges 10.12). Maon was probably in the hills of Judah.

Martyrs of the Early Church

Many of the leaders of the Early Church were martyred during the first century. Most of our information comes from sources outside the New Testament – Eusebius, the early Christian historian, for example, tells us that the Apostle Peter was crucified upside down in Rome during the persecutions of the emperor Nero, in about AD 64. However, the stoning of Stephen, the deacon, and the killing of James, the brother of John and son of Zebedee, are recounted in the New Testament (Acts 7.54–60 and Acts 12.1–3).
(see *Deacons* and *Disciples*)

Mary, Principal Individuals Named

There are five Marys to note particularly. Four are listed above under *Friends, Relations and Acquaintances of Jesus* – Mary of Bethany, Mary Magdalene, Mary, Mother of Jesus, and Mary, Wife of Clopas. The fifth receives only a very brief mention: 'As soon as he [Peter] realized this, he went to the house of Mary, the mother of John, whose other name was Mark, where many had gathered and were praying' (Acts 12.12).
(see *Evangelists* and *People of the Acts of the Apostles – John (Mark), Mary*)

77

Medes

The inhabitants of Media, an area south west of the Caspian Sea. They were, before the eighth century BC, semi-nomadic tribesmen who were beginning to settle throughout the area. Between the eighth and sixth centuries BC, they became a united force capable of harrying Assyria and finally, with the help of the Babylonians, conquering Nineveh in 612 BC. Cyrus the Great was an Elamite king and vassal of the king of the Medes, who rebelled and secured for himself the kingship of the empire of the Medes, later incorporating it into the larger Persian Empire.
(see *Elamites*)

Diagram
Map of the Fertile Crescent (5)

Midianites

Nomadic tribes who had descended from Abraham by his wife, Keturah (Genesis 25.2). They lived in northern Arabia; probably the Kenites were part of or closely associated with the Midianites. The Kenites were ultimately absorbed into Judah (Judges 1.16). Gideon defeated large numbers of Midianites mounted on camels but only after 'the Lord . . . [had given] them [the Israelites] into the hand of Midian for seven years' (Judges 6.1). Gideon's victory is recounted in Judges 7 and 8.
(see *Kenites*)

Mitannians

The inhabitants of the kingdom of Mitanni. It existed for about one hundred and thirty years between the Old Hittite Empire, and the New. The Mitannians were Hurrians who had arrived in Mesopotamia from the region of the Caucasian mountains.
(see *Amorites, Hittites* and *Hurrians*)

Diagrams
Map of the Fertile Crescent (5)
Broad Parallel Histories (16, 17)

Moabites

The descendants of Lot's son Moab, as the Ammonites were the descendants of Lot's son Ben-ammi. Originally, they were nomadic but eventually they settled in an area south east of the Dead Sea from which they seem to have ousted the Emim (Deuteronomy 2.10, 11) by about 1300 BC.

When the Israelites began their incursion, they avoided skirmishes with either the Moabites or the Ammonites because the two peoples had a secure grasp of their land and, in any event, they shared a common ancestry with the Israelites. However, they were eventually subjugated by King David.
(see *Ammonites*)

Diagrams
Family of Abraham (2)
Map of Canaan (6)

Nabateans

Semi-nomads who moved north from the western part of the Arabian Peninsula. They settled around Petra towards the end of the fourth century BC in the traditional lands of the Edomites who, anxious not to be assimilated, tended to move farther west into what became known as Idumea.
(see *Herods*)

Naphtali, Tribe of

The brother of Dan, sixth son of Jacob and the second by Bilhah. 'And Bilhah conceived and bore Jacob a son. Then Rachel said, "God has judged me, and has heard my voice and given me a son"; therefore she named him Dan' (Genesis 30.7, 8). The land allocated to the tribe of Naphtali was parallel with that of Asher, between Asher and the west of the Sea of Galilee, bordered by the Jordan north of Galilee (Joshua 19.30–39).

Diagrams
Children of Israel (3)
Tribal Lands of Israel (8)

Netophathites

Inhabitants of Netophah, a town near Bethlehem. Seraiah was a Netophathite who supported the appointment of Gedaliah as governor of Judah by Nebuchadnezzar (2 Kings 25.23).

Nomads and Semi-Nomads

When Abram (Abraham) and his relations left Ur in about 1750 BC (Genesis 11.31) they were, presumably, exchanging a sedentary existence for a nomadic or semi-nomadic life, and exchanging fixed dwellings for tents. Their movement was likely to have been associated in some way with the general movement of Semitic peoples throughout the land from the Arabian Desert and around the Fertile Crescent. The new life would involve pitching tent for a season and then moving on as the seasons and the herds demanded. They would gather food and trade their meat with the settled communities they discovered on their way. This life would continue from Haran and into Canaan, on to Egypt and back into Canaan before Abraham's grandson Jacob would take his family and settle for many generations in the land of Egypt. After the Exodus (*c*.1290 BC), the Israelites would once again become nomadic, a way of life they had left so long ago, until they were able to settle themselves permanently in the land of Canaan.
(see *Habiru*)

Patriarchs

Nubians
The inhabitants of Nubia, an area in north-east Africa in the Nile valley, dominated by Egypt from about 2000 BC to 750 BC.
(see *Cushites*)

Patriarchs

The Patriarchs, though strictly the heads of any of the numerous clans and families, have come to mean the heads of the first four generations of the Hebrews – Abraham, Isaac, Jacob and the twelve sons of Jacob. They feature in the various traditions and stories – some written, some oral – transmitted through very many centuries and finally combined to form the book of Genesis more or less as we know it, during the period after the return from exile in Babylon.

The stories of the Patriarchs give a grandeur and unflagging momentum to the great saga of the life of the Hebrews, while pointing back to the Creation, the disobedience of Adam, the emergence of Noah from the Great Flood, and so on. The stories of Genesis, and the following books, show God in action throughout history in the life of a nation, and show how human understanding of the nature of God gradually dawned.

(see *Children of Israel, Chosen People, Habiru* and *Hebrews*)

Abraham
The principal patriarch of the Israelites. (In Genesis 17.1–6 Abram is given the name, Abraham, possibly an Aramaic version of the same name. The writer of Genesis extends the meaning of the new name to show that Abraham was the ancestor of many nations, perhaps a figurehead for all mankind.) He lived with his family in Ur during a time of great upheaval in the region when many races were on the move around and into Mesopotamia. All scholars do not agree about the likely date but many find a date around 1750 BC acceptable. It is from this region that the ancient Garden of Eden and Flood stories originate.

From Ur the family moved to Haran, and then Abraham took his family south to Hebron and into the Negeb and, eventually, during a period of drought, to Egypt, a journey his grandson, Jacob, would make. Having returned to the region of Bethel, he agreed that he and Lot, his brother, should go their separate ways. God promised Abraham the land of Canaan and Sarah, late in life, produced a son, Isaac. To test Abraham's faith, God asked him to sacrifice his son, and then provided a ram for the purpose instead. This episode is probably a folk memory of the rejection of human sacrifice, which has been woven into the saga.

Isaac
The son of Abraham and father, by his cousin, Rebekah, of Esau and Jacob. Esau became the ancestor of the Edomites and Amelekites, and Jacob the father of the nation of Israel.

Jacob
Renamed Israel by God, he produced twelve sons by his wives, the two sisters Leah and Rachel, and their maids. These twelve sons became the ancestors of the twelve tribes of Israel. During a severe famine, Jacob took the whole extended family to Egypt where his son, Joseph, had reached a position of authority in the pharaoh's court. The story of Joseph's journey to Egypt, his rise to power and the journey of his brothers and father to Egypt is given at some length in Genesis 37–46.

Diagrams
Descent of Abraham (1)
Family of Abraham (2)
Children of Israel (3)

People of the Acts of the Apostles

The Acts of the Apostles was Luke's sequel to his Gospel; both books are likely to have been written in the AD 70s. Acts begins with the Ascension of Jesus (Acts 1.1–11) and the events of Pentecost (Acts 2). Between the two accounts, Matthias is chosen to replace Judas Iscariot as one of the Twelve. The rest of the book is concerned with the detail of the development of the Early Church – chapters 3–12 feature Peter, principally, and chapters 13–28 feature Paul as the principal character. It is believed that both men perished in Rome between AD 64 and AD 66 under the direction of the Emperor Nero.

There are many significant individuals featured in the book; some of them were great pillars of the Early Church (all the original disciples –the eleven – are noted in Acts 1.13), others were, perhaps, of less importance. It is worth recalling some of them along with the notable enemies of the Early Church.

Aeneus

Aeneus was a sick man, bedridden for eight years, whom Peter cured during a visit to Lydda (Acts 9.32–35).

Ananias

There are three so named. The first is the character in a moral story about dishonesty and lack of openness included by Luke to complement the report of Barnabas' generosity in the previous verses (Acts 5.1–11). The second was a disciple in Damascus who was instrumental in the recovery of Paul's sight (Acts 9.10–18). The third is the name of the high priest who, when Paul was taken before the council, ordered Paul to be struck on the mouth (Acts 23.2).

Apollos

A Christian Jew who 'spoke with burning enthusiasm to whom Priscilla and Aquila explained the Way of God . . . more accurately'. In Achaia 'he greatly helped those who through grace had become believers' (Acts 18.24–28).

Aquila and Priscilla

Jewish Christians who had settled in Ephesus (Acts 18.1–4 and 24–26).

Aristarchus

A Christian who accompanied Paul from time to time (Acts 20.4).

Bar-Jesus

He tried to hinder the conversion of the proconsul, Sergius Paulus, and was temporarily blinded for his trouble (Acts 13.4–12).

Barnabas

A Christian Jew from Cyprus. He introduced the newly converted Paul to the apostles in Jerusalem (Acts 9.27).

People of the Acts of the Apostles

Cornelius
He was persuaded in a vision that he should send for Peter to preach in Caesarea. He was 'a centurion of the Italian Cohort' (Acts 10.1–8).

Crispus
The 'official of the synagogue' in Corinth who became a Christian (Acts 18.8).

Damaris
While in Athens Paul converted a number of people 'including Dionysius the Areopagite and a woman named Damaris, and others with them' (Acts 17.34).

Dionysius
(see *Damaris*)

Dorcas
A disciple whom Peter restored to life after he had been told about her acts of charity (Acts 9.36–43). Dorcas is the Greek form of Tabitha.

Eutychus
He fell asleep while Paul talked at some length, and promptly fell to the ground out of a window. Paul revived him (Acts 20.9–12).

Felix
The governor of Judea between AD 52 and AD 60. He imprisoned Paul in Caesarea from about AD 58 to AD 60 (Acts 24.22–27).

Festus
He succeeded Felix as governor and sent Paul to Agrippa (Acts 25 and 26).

Gallio
It was before Gallio that Paul was taken because he was 'persuading people to worship God in ways that are contrary to the law' (Acts 18.13). Gallio told the Jews to sort matters out for themselves.

Gamaliel
The Pharisee who objected to the killing of the apostles (Acts 5.33–42).

James I
This James was the disciple of Jesus and brother of John the beloved disciple. Herod Agrippa had James put to death (Acts 12.1, 2).
(see *Disciples* and *Martyrs*)

James III
This James, the 'brother' of Jesus was leader or bishop of the Jerusalem church, and may have been the author of the Letter of James (Acts 21.17–20).
(see *Brothers of Jesus*)

Jason
A Christian in whose house in Thessalonica Paul and Silas received hospitality. A mob attacked the house in its search for Paul and Silas (Acts 17.5–8).

John
The beloved disciple, who accompanied Peter in the early days of ministry (Acts 3 and 4).
(see *Disciples*)

John (Mark)
It is likely that John Mark wrote the Gospel of Mark and that he wrote it largely from Peter's own reminiscences. He was a companion of both Paul and Barnabas, and may have accompanied Peter to Rome (Acts 12.12).
(see *Evangelists*)

Judas Barsabbas
This Judas was sent with Silas to join Paul and Barnabas in Antioch (Acts 15.22).

Mary
This Mary was Peter's friend and mother of John Mark (Acts 12.12).

Matthias
He accompanied the disciples during Jesus' ministry and became the twelfth disciple in place of Judas Iscariot (Acts 1.21–26).
(see *Apostles* and *Disciples*)

Paul (Saul)
A persecutor of Christians who was converted (Acts 9) to become a most zealous missionary and apostle of the Church (Acts 9–28).
(see *Apostles,* and *Letter Writers of the New Testament*)

Peter
The principal spokesman for the Early Church (Acts 1.15 and 2.14 etc.). He had received the special commission from Jesus himself.
(see *Apostles,* and *Disciples*)

Philip
This was Philip the deacon, who baptized the Ethiopian eunuch (Acts 8.26- 40).
(see *Deacons*)

Priscilla
The wife of Aquila (Acts 18.1–4, 24–26).

Publius
The 'leading man of the island' of Malta when Paul visited. Publius' father, who lay sick, was prayed over and cured by Paul (Acts 28.7–10).

People of the Acts of the Apostles

Rhoda
She was so excited at seeing Peter (who had escaped from prison) she omitted to invite him into the house when she answered the door (Acts 12.12-17).

Sapphira
(see *Ananias (1)*)

Sceva
The name of the Jewish priest whose seven sons tried unsuccessfully to perform exorcisms by saying 'over those who had evil spirits, "I adjure you by the Jesus whom Paul proclaims"' (Acts 19.11–20).

Sergius Paulus
He was converted through the efforts of Paul and Barnabas.
(see *Bar-Jesus*)

Silas
Silas (sometimes named Silvanus in the epistles) and Judas Barsabbas were sent to join Paul and Barnabas in Antioch (Acts 15).

Simon
There are two Simons to consider: Simon 'who previously practised magic . . . in the city of Samaria' (Acts 8.9) and who was baptized by Philip (Acts 8.13); and Simon the tanner with whom Peter stayed in Joppa (Acts 9.43).

Sosthenes
This is not the co-writer of the first letter to the Corinthians. This man was 'the official of the synagogue' (Acts 18.17) beaten by the Jews before Gallio. Presumably, Sosthenes wished to give Paul a fair hearing.

Stephen
(see *Martyrs*)

Tabitha
(see *Dorcas*)

Timothy
A faithful companion to Paul throughout many of his missionary journeys (Acts 16.1–5).

Tychicus
Tychicus was one of the companions to Paul and Luke when they sailed to Macedonia (Acts 20.4).

People of the Babylonian Captivity and Return

Cyrus the Great (see *Kings of Other Lands*)

Ezekiel (see *Prophets – Ezekiel*)

Ezra (see *Priests –Ezra* and *Writers of the Old Testament – Ezra*)

Haggai (see *Prophets – Haggai*)

Isaiah II (see *Prophets – Isaiah II*)

Jeremiah (see *Prophets – Jeremiah*)

Jeshua (see *Priests – Jeshua*)

Nebuchadnezzar (see *Kings of Other Lands*)

Nehemiah (see *Writers of the Old Testament*)

Zechariah (see *Prophets – Zechariah*)

Zerubbabel
A descendant of the royal line of David, who led the first phase of the return to Jerusalem from exile in Babylon.

Cyrus the Great overran Babylon in 538 BC, and allowed the Jews to return to Jerusalem with the temple vessels stolen by Nebuchadnezzar. Zerubbabel and Jeshua the priest returned to Jerusalem in order to begin the work of the rebuilding of the temple and the city. The work, though supported by the prophets Haggai and Zechariah, had lost its impetus by 500 BC, and it was left to Ezra to lead a more vital expedition of reconstruction in about 458 BC and, with Nehemiah as Governor of Jerusalem (445–433 BC) succeeded in restoring Judah but with a firmly established high priesthood rather than a monarchy. (However, some scholars suggest Ezra's mission was after Nehemiah's governorship, in 398 BC.) (Ezra and Nehemiah) (see *Babylonians* and *Persians*)

Diagram
Broad Parallel Histories (22)

People of the Letters of the New Testament (not mentioned in Acts)

Many of those who are mentioned in the letters are also mentioned in the Acts of the Apostles; some are not and it is worth noting just a few of them.

Archippus
At the end of the Letter to the Colossians, the writer gives Archippus a nudge – 'See that you complete the task that you have received in the Lord' (Colossians 4.18). Archippus is also addressed in the opening greeting of Paul's letter to Philemon.

Demas

He is numbered among Paul's fellow workers at the end of his letter to Philemon. He is mentioned in a pejorative way at the end of the second letter to Timothy (2 Timothy 4.9).

Epaphras

Paul's fellow prisoner at one time (Philemon 23).

Epaphroditus

A fellow worker of Paul's mentioned in the letter Paul wrote from prison in Ephesus to the Philippians (Philippians 2.25; 4.18).

Onesimus

The slave who assisted Paul in prison. He was the subject of Paul's letter to Philemon.

Philemon

A Christian to whom Paul wrote about the slave, Onesimus.

Sosthenes

The co-writer, though probably a subordinate one, of Paul's first letter to the Corinthians.

Titus

An important companion to Paul, who featured in the second letter to the Corinthians (2 Corinthians 8.6; 12.18).
(see *Letter Writers of the New Testament*)

Perezites

The clan of Perez, son of Judah (Numbers 26.20).

Perizzites

They numbered among the peoples encountered by the Israelites as they began their entry into Canaan. It is difficult to place the Perizzites with any precision but in one reference they seem to be located in the highlands north of the tribal land of Ephraim in what would in the future become Samaria (Joshua 17.15).

Persians

It was Cyrus the Great who brought the Persians into prominence. Cyrus was the king of the minor city-state of Anshan in Elam. Anshan was within the Median Empire and under its control. It seems that Cyrus rebelled against the king of the Medes and in a very short time had usurped the king and, within three years, had assumed control over the Median Empire. He now titled himself King of the Persians. With remarkable speed and efficiency Cyrus soon enveloped Lydia and then moved eastwards before returning to take Babylonia, in 539 BC, which hardly resisted.

The Persians ultimately embraced a vast empire from Scythia in the east to

Macedonia, on the threshold of Greece, in the west. Its western possessions included Libya and Egypt. It was not until some two hundred years after Cyrus had entered Babylonia that the Persian Empire succumbed to the force, determination and speed of Alexander the Great. Persian control of Judah came to an end in 332 BC. One of Cyrus's first acts was to decree that Jerusalem would be rebuilt and the captives in Babylon permitted to return. (Ezra and Nehemiah)

It is helpful to glance at the complete list of Persian kings in association with this article and that of the *People of the Babylonian Captivity and Return.*

Cyrus the Great	560–530 BC
Cambyses	530–522
Bardiya	522
Darius I	522–486
Xerxes I (Ahasuerus)	486–465
(see *Writers of the Old Testament – Esther*)	
Artaxerxes I	465–424
Xerxes II	424
Sogdianos	424–423
Darius II	423–404
Artaxerxes II	404–358
Artaxerxes III	358–337
Artaxerxes IV	337–336
Darius III	336–330

Pharaohs

(see *Egyptians* and *Kings of Other Lands*)

Pharisees

The two main sects of Judaism to emerge after the Seleucid period of control in Judea and during the Maccabean period were the Sadducees and the Pharisees. The Pharisees are difficult to define. In the writings about them, they appear to be a lay elite concerned with a precise interpretation of the written law and of the oral law. They accepted resurrection (unlike the Sadducees) and had firm belief in the spiritual world. The writers of the Gospels point to the Pharisees as examples of the blindness and hypocrisy that can be the result of an overzealous application of the niceties of the law.

Philippians

The people of Philippi, in Macedonia. Paul wrote, in about AD 55, to the Christians there, while he was imprisoned in Ephesus.

Philistines

The inhabitants of the coastal region of southern Palestine. They were the sea peoples who had harried the Egyptians and who eventually began to settle. They may have come from many places in and around the Mediterranean Sea. At least one of the Philistine gods – the goddess Ashdoda – seems to hail from the Mycenaean civilization that overcame the Cretan Minoans around 1400 BC.

Phoenicians

The Philistines were a constant threat to the Israelites as they left exile in Egypt and entered and settled in Canaan. During the period of the judge Shamgar, there were successes against the Philistines. 'After him [Ehud] came Shamgar, son of Anath, who killed six hundred of the Philistines with an ox-goad' (Judges 3.31). Later, the Samson stories are mainly concerned with the Philistines (Judges 13–16). The two books of Samuel contain many references to war with the Philistines, perhaps the most notable is the contest between David and the Philistine champion, Goliath, during the reign of Saul (1 Samuel 17.1–54). They continued to be a source of trouble into the period of the divided monarchy. They succumbed to Assyrian domination in 701 BC and were finally annihilated by Nebuchadnessar in 604 BC. The five cities of the Philistines were: Ashdod, Ashkelon, Ekron, Gaza and Gath.

Phoenicians

They were probably Amorites who had settled in the islands off the coast and into the mainland in a group of city-states from about the beginning of the second millennium. The most important of these city-states were Tyre and Sidon, which were then joined to the coast by causeways. King Hiram of Tyre was a close ally of King Solomon (1 Kings 5). Other Phoenician city-states were Ugarit, Arvad and Byblos. Generally speaking, the Phoenicians are referred to in the Bible as Sidonians.

In the ninth century BC, the Phoenicians succumbed to the might of the Assyrians.

Diagram
Map of the Fertile Crescent (5)

Pirathonites

The inhabitants of Pirathon, which was the home of Abdon, the judge of Israel (Judges 12.13, 14).

Priests and High Priests

The complex history and development of the Israelite priesthood is best considered in the light of some of the individuals who held the office. In simple terms, the tribe of Levi was designated as the functional tribe responsible for all priestly duties. It was from this line that Aaron had come, and his family provided the principal or chief priests until Solomon appointed Zadok and his heirs to the task. The temple-based work of the priesthood was brought to an end when the temple at Jerusalem was destroyed. The office of High Priest seems to be a creation belonging to the period after the return to Jerusalem from Babylon. It is certainly of importance from this time but the position is suggested in Joshua 20.6.

Aaron
The brother of Moses; and together theirs was the responsibility to lead the Israelites from slavery and into the wilderness to prepare for the conquest of Canaan. The description of the manner in which vestments were to be made and priests were to be ordained is contained in Exodus chapters 28 and 29. Despite acquiescing to the people's demand for a golden calf while Moses is on Mount Sinai, Aaron is consecrated priest and vestments made 'for the priest Aaron . . . and his sons to serve as priests' (Exodus 39.41)
(see *Aaronites*)

Abiathar
He was probably the last in the line of Aaronite priests, and the son of Ahimelech. Abiathar supported the claim to the throne by David's son, Adonijah. When Solomon succeeded, he deprived Abiathar of his priestly function and replaced him with the priest, Zadok (1 Kings 2.26–35).

Abinadab
He carried out the priestly function of housing the sacred ark, which had been returned by the Philistines, in his home at Kiriath-jearim. 'They consecrated his son, Eleazar, to have charge of the ark of the Lord' (1 Samuel 7.1).

The ark remained at Kiriath-jearim for twenty years until David took it with much ceremony to Jerusalem.

Ahimelech
The father of Abiathar. He was killed by Doeg the Edomite, on the orders of Saul, for supporting David. On that day eighty-five priests were killed (1 Samuel 22.16–19).

Alexander Janneus
The Maccabean high priest (and king) 104–76 BC.

Ananias
The high priest who ordered those at the council in Jerusalem to strike Paul on the mouth (Acts 23.1, 2).

Annas
High priest in Jerusalem until AD 15 and then succeeded by various members of his family. At the time of Jesus' arrest, his son-in-law, Caiaphas, was high priest. In John's Gospel, the writer records that Jesus was taken first to Annas, and then to Caiaphas (Luke 3.2 and John 18.19–24).

Eleazar
Eleazar I was the son of Aaron, who succeeded him in priestly office. He was the companion of Joshua (Joshua 14.1).

Eleazar II was the son of Abinadab and consecrated to perform the priestly function of guardian of the ark.
(see *Abinadab*)

Eli
The priest at Shiloh who encouraged Samuel (his 'adopted' apprentice, as it were) to listen to what God was saying to him. It was from Shiloh that the ark was stolen by the Philistines, after their success in battle against the Israelites. Eli's sons, Hophni and Phineas, were killed in the battle. Eli, an old man, died after hearing news of the battle (1 Samuel 4.17, 18).
(see *Abinadab*)

Ezra
The priest who masterminded one of the phases of the return from exile, either in 458 BC before Nehemiah's first mission between 445 BC and 443 BC, or afterwards, in

Priests and High Priests

398 BC. The difficulty springs from Ezra 7.1. Does the text refer to Artaxerxes I or II? Perhaps the earlier date is more usually preferred.
(see *People of the Babylonian Captivity and Return*)

Hilkiah
The father of Jeremiah the prophet, and a priest at Jerusalem in the reign of King Josiah. He was responsible for rediscovering in the temple what was the core of the Book of Deuteronomy. He set in motion reforms that would fuel the interests and enthusiasms of the reformers in exile, and would, ultimately, be the base of the new constitution after the return (2 Kings 22, 23.1–30).

Hyrcanus
Hyrcanus I was the Maccabean high priest (and king) 134–104 BC
Hyrcanus II was the Maccabean high priest 76–67 BC and again in 63 BC.

Ithamar
The fourth son of Aaron and called to serve as priest (Exodus 28.1).

Jehoiada
The priest who revealed that Joash had been saved from the massacre instigated by Athaliah (2 Kings 11.4–12).
(see *Kings of the Kingdom of Judah*)

Jeshua
The priest who accompanied Zerubbabel on the first phase of the return to Jerusalem (Ezra and Haggai 1).
(see *People of the Babylonian Captivity and Return – Zerubbabel*)

Jonathan
The Maccabean high priest 160–142 BC.

Melchizedek
King Melchizedek of Salem was the mysterious 'priest of God Most High' (Genesis 14.18–20) who gave Abram (Abraham) sustenance after he had succeeded against the four kings.

Meremoth
The most senior of a band of priests who returned to Jerusalem with Ezra (Ezra 8.33).

Phineas
Phineas I was the grandson of Aaron and son of Eleazar (Joshua 24.33).
Phineas II was one of the sons of Eli killed in the battle with the Philistines.

Simon
The Maccabean high priest 140–134 BC. He succeeded his brother Jonathan. Both were brothers of Judas.

Zadok

The priest who, together with Nathan the prophet, was instrumental in ensuring the succession of Solomon as king, on the death of David. Solomon made Zadok chief priest and deposed Abiathar (1 Kings 2.35).

Zechariah

The husband of Elizabeth and father of John the Baptist (Luke 1).

Principal People of the Exodus, the Wilderness and Entry into Canaan

Moses, Aaron, Miriam, Joshua and Caleb

When there rose up a new king over Egypt – probably Ahmose (although some scholars assert that the pharaoh in question was more likely to have been Seti I, some two hundred years later) – 'who did not know Joseph' (Exodus 1.8), the Israelites were enslaved. Moses was commissioned by God to extricate the Israelites from Egypt. This he did with cunning and divine intervention, and with the help of his brother, Aaron, and sister, Miriam. The Israelites escaped to the wilderness where they waited to enter Canaan. During this time, God gave his law to Moses.

The Israelites complained bitterly about their nomadic existence, something they had given up hundreds of years before, and about the general discomforts of life. They even turned from God and worshipped a golden calf. God was angry at their ingratitude and unfaithfulness and refused to allow this whole generation, along with Moses and Aaron, to enter Canaan, east of the Jordan. They died before the river Jordan was crossed. Of all the Israelites who had fled from Egypt, only Joshua and his right hand man, Caleb, crossed both the Red Sea and the river Jordan to enter the land of Canaan. (Exodus, Numbers, Deuteronomy and Joshua)

(see *Aaronites, Children of Israel, Kings of Other Lands – Ahmose, Rameses II* and *Seti I* and *Writers of the Old Testament – Exodus*)

Diagrams
Tree of the Tribe of Levi (4)
Map of the Route of the Exodus (7)
Broad Parallel Histories (16, 17)

Prophets of the Old Testament

The prophets were the consciences of Israel (later, Israel and Judah); the men who tried to encourage kings and officials and the people generally, to return to the ways of moral and spiritual uprightness. They flourished from the days of Samuel to the days of the return to Jerusalem from Babylon, and on to John the Baptist, who can rightly be termed the last of the Old Testament-style prophets.

When the prophets saw the moral and spiritual decline around them, they foresaw the, sometimes dire, consequences of a failure to return to the ways of righteousness. The prophets interpreted the state of the nation as they saw it: some were also politicians and often were instrumental in putting into effect what they considered necessary action, even if it meant taking up the sword themselves; some spoke merely to prompt; others offered the strength of an encouraging message of God to his people. All prophets – even those who took 'direct action' – were capable of standing back from events to take stock of the situation, and to consider. Above all, the true prophet had a God-given vocation, and was inspired to be a prophet. Even the true prophet was sometimes reluctant to accept God's commission.

The pronouncements of the prophets reveal gradually and build up a picture of something of the nature of God – for example: he is the only God (Amos); he is a holy and transcendent God (Isaiah); he is a just God who deals squarely with people (Amos); he is a loving and forgiving God (Hosea).

There is no substitute for reading and re-reading the passages in the bible in which each prophet is featured, but it is of use to note here one or two characteristics or circumstances of each of the principal prophets, and at least the names of the lesser prophets. The books of the Old Testament that bear the names of prophets are divided into: (1) Major Prophets – Isaiah, Jeremiah and Ezekiel; (2) Minor Prophets – Hosea, Joel, Amos, Obadiah, Jonah, Micah, Nahum, Habakkuk, Zephaniah, Haggai, Zechariah and Malachi.

Ahijah

Ahijah was the prophet from Shiloh who talked to Jeroboam on the road from Jerusalem and after tearing his own coat into twelve pieces (representing the twelve tribes of Israel) asked Jeroboam to select ten. Ahijah thus predicted the division of the kingdom into Israel and Judah because Solomon had begun to entertain the worship of Phoenician gods. Jeroboam was to become the king of the northern kingdom of Israel (1 Kings 11.29–33).

Amos

Amos operated for a short time in the northern kingdom of Israel in about the middle of the eighth century BC. Amos foresees the destruction of the northern kingdom as a consequence of the religious, social and moral degradation of the country. However, he sees that the God of the Israelites is the only God, and, therefore, the God of all nations; a God who deals justly with all his people. The destruction of Israel at the hand of the Assyrians occurred about thirty years later (Amos).

Daniel

The books of Daniel (some of which – *The Prayer of Azariah and the Song of the Three Young Men, Susanna* and *Bel and the Dragon* – appear in the Apocrypha in some versions of the Bible) comprise a number of stories of very different types. Daniel in Babylon is concerned with faithfulness to God and with the power of God; later we find apocalyptic literature, a moral tale about Susanna, and a story about seventy priests of Bel, and a dragon. The books contain elements of the prophet's art and prophecy it is true, but Daniel is really a character of the story-teller's art created to deliver a particular message. The stories were collected during the Maccabean period in the second century BC.

Deborah

One of the judges of Israel but was also a prophetess. In Judges 4.5, she appears as an oracle or soothsayer rather than a prophet in the sense with which we are dealing in this section (Judges 4, 5).

Eli

The prophet and priest at Shiloh whom Samuel succeeded. He was a holy and venerable man but two of his sons – Hophni and Phinehas – were somewhat dishonest in their dealings with the temple funds (1 Samuel 1–4).

Elijah

He was certainly one of the active prophets as is demonstrated in the story of the four hundred and fifty priests of Baal called to a contest by Elijah (1 Kings 18.17–40). Elijah was a thorn in the flesh of Ahab, king of Israel who had married Jezebel, the daughter of the Sidonian king, and had imported certain heathen practices from the Sidonians. Elijah anointed Elisha his successor (1 Kings 17–2 Kings 2.12).

Elisha

·Elijah's successor. Many miracles are attributed to him and he seems to have been responsible, at length, for a whole band of prophets. His prime duty was to make sure that Jehu was anointed king in order to bring an end to the dynasty of Ahab and the unfaithfulness to God that that dynasty had brought about. Elisha sent a member of the company of prophets to carry out this duty on his behalf (2 Kings 2.13–13.21).

Ezekiel

A prophet who had been transported to Babylon in 597 BC or ten years later during the second transportation. There is much curious imagery in the book but he clearly deals with the rebellion against the ways of God of the whole nation of Israel (i.e. both Israel and Judah). In the end he prophesies that the nations can be reborn and recover, and be restored as one. Chapter 37 of his book describes the vision of the valley of the dry bones, perhaps the best-known passage of Ezekiel (Ezekiel).

Habakkuk

He flourished just before the end of the seventh century BC (after the fall of Nineveh) in Judah during the period immediately before the first of the transportations to Babylon. The short book is prayerful (Habakkuk).

Haggai

Haggai can be dated around 520 BC. He was an ardent supporter of the return to Jerusalem and of the reconstruction of the temple. He saw the re-establishment of the temple priesthood as an essential focus for the rebirth of the nation (Haggai, Ezra 5.1).

Hosea

A prophet of about the mid-eighth century BC in the northern kingdom of Israel. He knew where Israel's unfaithfulness would lead. Assyria's intentions were clear to most. However, Hosea asserted, as a husband is able to forgive an unfaithful wife, so God would punish and forgive (Hosea).

Isaiah

Contained in the book of Isaiah are three Isaiahs.

The prophecies of Isaiah I are contained in Isaiah 1–39. He was a prophet and had the ear of four kings of Judah during the second half of the eighth century BC – from Azariah (Uzziah) to Hezekiah. The book of Isaiah I contains visions, poetry, straightforward comment on the evil ways of mankind, political comment and messages of hope for the future. But only after the sin of the nation is properly punished would the divine promise be fulfilled. Isaiah gives us those glorious pictures of the Messiah, particularly in chapter 35. Isaiah reveals to us the holiness and transcendence and God (Isaiah 1–39; 2 Kings 19–20).

The prophecies of Isaiah II are contained in Isaiah 40–55. This prophet is unnamed but we may date him around the time of Cyrus's conquest of Babylon. He gives us those famous words of comfort and the promise of a forerunner. 'A voice cries out: "In the wilderness prepare the way of the Lord, make straight in the desert a highway for our God."' (Isaiah 40.3) (Isaiah 40–55).

The prophecies of Isaiah III are contained in Isaiah 56–66. This prophet is also unnamed but we may place him among those who returned to Jerusalem from Babylon. His utterances are poetic and, from time to time, prayerful. From this Isaiah comes the call: 'Arise, shine; for your light has come, and the glory of the Lord has risen upon you' (Isaiah 60.1) (Isaiah 56–66).

Jeremiah
He lived from the time of King Josiah's reforms (Hilkiah, Jeremiah's father had found what was probably the Book of Deuteronomy in the temple (see *Priests – Hilkiah*)) to a period after Nebuchadnezzar's governor, Gedaliah, was murdered in Jerusalem. He ended his days in Egypt. He foresaw the destruction of Jerusalem by Babylon as an instrument of God purging his people for their grave misdemeanours. Jeremiah is unlikely, it is now thought, to have been the writer of Lamentations (Jeremiah).

Joel
His prophecies probably date from about 350 BC, though this is by no means certain. His book contains much about repentance and God's promise for the future. If the date is correct, this was the time when Judah was formed into a theocratic state, but within the Persian Empire under Artaxerxes III (Joel).

John the Baptist
Quite properly, John is usually considered the last of the Old Testament-style prophets. Indeed he associates himself with the words of Isaiah II and, for that matter, Malachi, and seems to have the appearance of Elijah (2 Kings 1.8). His only functions are to prepare people for the coming of the Messiah and to point the way to him. But he is a prophet with a difference because he is able, literally, to point to Jesus as he says: 'This is the Lamb of God who takes away the sin of the world! This is he of whom I said, "After me comes a man who ranks ahead of me because he was before me."' (John 1.29, 30).
(Matthew 3, Mark 1, Luke 3, John 1)
(see *Family of John the Baptist* and *Family of Jesus*)

Jonah
There are, perhaps, two Jonahs.

Jonah I lived in the reign of Jeroboam II of Israel and he is mentioned only fleetingly in the passage concerning that king (2 Kings 14.25).

Jonah II is the hero of a homily written between, say, 450 and 350 BC. It may be that old legends about the earlier prophet have been reworked to form this worthy teaching narrative (Jonah).

Malachi

The writer of Malachi is unknown – the name simply means 'my messenger'. The writer shows interest in the concepts of repentance, judgement, forgiveness, and the coming of the Lord. He foresees a forerunner: 'See, I am sending my messenger to prepare the way before me, and the Lord whom you seek will suddenly come to his temple' (Malachi 3.1). He uses the didactic technique of introducing his arguments with a question. The book probably dates from the first half of the fifth century BC.

Micah

Micah's introduction places him around the time of Isaiah I. Micah's prophecies promise God's forgiveness and hope; and he stresses the need for purity of worship. He foresees captivity and restoration for the remnant. 'But you, O Bethlehem of Ephrathah, who are one of the little clans of Judah, from you shall come forth for me one who is to rule in Israel, whose origin is from old, from ancient days' (Micah 5.2) (Micah).

Micaiah

The only prophet among his fellows in Israel to disagree with the course of action that they proposed. He warned against an encounter with Aram and was placed in custody. In the battle King Ahab died (1 Kings 22.5–28).

Nahum

Nahum's prophetic utterances against Assyria explode from every verse. Nahum can see the inevitability of Assyria's downfall and rejoices in it. This places Nahum's prophecy around the time of the fall of Nineveh in 612 BC. He probably lived in Judah (Nahum).

Nathan

He was instrumental in gaining for Solomon the throne of his father. He accompanied Zadok the priest to the anointing of Solomon (1 Kings 1).

Obadiah

The writings contained in Obadiah seem to come from the time of the Babylonian capture of Jerusalem in 597 BC. The theme is the judgement and justice of defeat, and hope for the future. (Obadiah)

Zechariah

This work dates from the period of the return from exile in about 520 BC. The first six chapters contain Zechariah's eight visions; chapters seven and eight, the word from God. (Chapters 9–14 of the book are a later addition, probably by about two hundred years, containing messages of messianic hope, including the passage in 9.9 cited (John 12.15) at Jesus' entry into Jerusalem. 'Lo, your king comes to you; triumphant and victorious is he, humble and riding on a donkey, on a colt, the foal of a donkey'.) Ezra 5.1 places Zechariah with Haggai. He was, therefore, an ardent supporter of the rebuilding of Jerusalem and its temple (Zechariah, Ezra 5.1).

Zephaniah

Zephaniah's prophecy dates from early in the reign of King Josiah of Judah and before the reforms of Josiah, which were prompted by Hilkiah's finding what was the core of the Book of Deuteronomy in the temple. Zephaniah's themes are that judgement will be given to those who have been unfaithful to God; that judgement will extend to the surrounding nations; that hope awaits those who remain faithful to God (Zephaniah).

Ptolemys

The dynasty of the Ptolemys sprang from the general to whom was allotted one third of the Alexandrian Empire on the death of Alexander. At first, the Ptolemaic Empire embraced Libya, Egypt and Palestine from 305 BC to 198 BC when Ptolemy V lost Palestine to the Seleucid Empire.
(see *Greeks, Grecians and Hellenists*)

Rabbis

The rabbis – i.e. ordained scholars holding office – did not exist before the period after the destruction of the temple in AD 70. Indeed, the form of address, 'rabbi', was not known before the first century AD. In that century before about AD 70 and in the Gospels – the term is not used in the Gospel of Luke – it is used as a courtesy title and an address of respect meaning, 'my master'. It is used by the disciples of Jesus in the Gospel of Mark; only by Judas Iscariot in the Gospel of Matthew; and, in the Gospel of John, by the disciples and, occasionally, by others.

Reuben, Tribe of

Reuben was the first son born to Jacob, and was the ancestor of the tribe of Reuben. 'When the Lord saw that Leah was unloved, he opened her womb ... Leah conceived and bore a son, and she named him Reuben' (Genesis 29.31, 32). The land allocated to the tribe of Reuben was an area north east of the Dead Sea, and north of the land of Gad (Joshua 13.15–23).

Diagrams
Children of Israel (3)
Tribal Lands of Israel (8)

Romans

The addressees of one of Paul's letters.
(see *Letter Writers of the New Testament – Romans*)

In the New Testament the term, Romans, variously identified those who lived in Rome, were born there, or were citizens of Rome.

The term is also used nowadays as a synonym for the Roman Empire. The long arm of the Roman Empire reached Palestine in 63 BC when Pompey entered Jerusalem. The independent state of Maccabean Judea was in disarray and Rome had already overcome the countries around the Mediterranean where once had ruled the successors of Alexander's great empire.

Hyrcanus, the brother of King Aristobulus II, the last king of the Maccabean dynasty, was appointed high priest in charge of Judea in 63 BC; and Julius Caesar himself made Antipas, the father of Herod the Great, governor of Judea. In 47 BC, Herod the Great was made governor of Galilee and, from 37 BC, king of Judea. Augustus then divided the country among Herod's sons and, anxious that there should be a greater Roman influence and presence in Palestine, appointed a series of governors, or procurators, to enforce Roman law while allowing the Jews autonomy in domestic and religious matters under the high priest. No matter how this was presented, the fact remained – and it was now made more apparent – that the Jews were again under the heel of a foreign and pagan invader.

(The charge of blasphemy against Jesus was clearly not going to be sufficiently grave to have the case placed before the Roman Governor, but a charge that he claimed to be the Messiah and was, therefore, by extension, rebellious and potentially treasonous and seditious, was ideal for the purposes of the religious leaders who wished to be rid of Jesus, even if it meant using the power of the hated occupiers of their land. The Roman governor at the time of Jesus' trial and crucifixion was Pontius Pilate (Matthew 27; Mark 15; Luke 23; John 18, 19).)

The Herodian dynasty expired with the death of Agrippa II, king of Chalcis, AD 48–100.
(see *Herods*)

Roman Emperors

(Julius Caesar etc.)
(Julius Caesar 49–44 BC)
(Mark Antony etc.)
(Octavius etc, (Octavius became first emperor and adopted the name Augustus))
Augustus 27 BC–AD 14
Tiberius AD 14–37
Caligula AD 37–41
Claudius AD 41–54
Nero AD 54–68
Galba etc. AD 68–69
Vespasian AD 69–79
Titus AD 79–81
Domitian AD 81–96

Roman Governors or Procurators of Judea (to AD 41) and Palestine (from AD 44)

Coponius AD 6–9
Ambibulus AD 9–12
Rufus AD 12–15
Gratus AD 15–26
Pontius Pilate AD 26–36
Marullus AD 37
Capito AD 37–41
Fadus AD 44–46
Alexander AD 46–52
Felix AD 52–60
Festus AD 60–62
Albinus AD 62–64
Florus AD 64–66

Sadducees

A sect generally associated with the rich and the priestly elite. They were concerned with the written law but had no interest in the oral law beloved of the Pharisees. The Sadducees did not believe in the resurrection of the dead and it was on that subject that the Sadducees tested Jesus in their question concerning a much-married woman: 'Last of all, the woman herself died. In the resurrection, then, whose wife of the seven will she be?' (Matthew 22.27, 28).

Samaritans

The inhabitants of Samaria. The overthrow of Samaria by Assyria in 722 BC sealed the fate of the northern kingdom of Israel. Those who remained in Samaria – i.e. those who were not transported to Nineveh – grew,to look upon themselves as the remnant of the ten northern tribes of Israel.

The Samaritans were not considered by those who returned from Babylon to restore the temple at Jerusalem, as true holders of the faith. After all, they had mixed and intermarried with those Assyrians transported from Assyria to Samaria after the destruction of the northern kingdom. No, they could not assist in the reconstruction of Jerusalem (Ezra 4.1–4). This rejection may have been the beginning of the enmity between Jew and Samaritan, touched on frequently in the Gospels. Jesus instructed his disciples not to go to Samaria (Matthew 10.5, 6) but only a Samaritan thanks Jesus after the miracle of the Ten Lepers (Luke 17.11–19) and a Samaritan is the hero in the parable of The Good Samaritan (Luke 10.29–37). But in the Seleucid period, it seems that the Samaritans' holy place on Mount Gerizim was destroyed by John Hyrcanus, the Maccabean king and high priest, in about 111 BC.
(see *Maccabees*)

Scribes

The scribes are often associated with the Pharisees in the Gospels and, more often than not, they are shown to be enemies of Jesus. Their strength in the interpretation of the law and scripture generally was a skill they had developed after the fall of Jerusalem and their removal to Babylon. Ezra was one such.

Before the captivity, scribes had largely been bookkeepers and civil servants (1 Kings 4.1–4).

Scythians

These nomadic, mounted archers from the north beyond Assyria were troubling that empire in the second half of the seventh century. They poured into Mesopotamia from the other side of the Caucasus mountain range and contributed to the general unsettling and disintegration of Assyria. The Medes, who were becoming ever stronger in present-day Iran, drove them back over the mountains where they remained for a spell. The Medes then disposed of Assyria with the defeat of Nineveh, assisted by the Babylonians. The Scythians reappear long after the defeat of Nineveh, aiding the Persians in their defeat of Babylon in 538 BC.
(see *Assyrians* and *Babylonians*)

Sea Peoples

(see *Philistines*) .

Seleucids

(see *Greeks, Grecians and Hellenists*)

Semites

The writers of Genesis saw themselves as just a part of the whole table of nations contained in chapters 10 and 11. The legendary Noah was responsible for repopulating the earth after the flood, and his firstborn, Shem, was the ancestor of the inhabitants of most of the countries surrounding Israel, and, of course, Israel itself. (Shem was the great-grandfather of Eber, the father of the Hebrews (Genesis 11.10–26).) These were, therefore, the Semites, though the name does not appear in the Bible. (see *Habiru, Hebrews* and *Writers of the Old Testament*)

Diagram
Descent of Abraham (1)

Shechemites

Shechem was the son of Jacob's neighbour, the prince of the city of Shechem (Genesis 33.18–20). The Shechemites were the inhabitants of the city.

In chapter 34 of Genesis, we read the intriguing story of the slaughter of the Shechemite males by Simeon and Levi, on account of Shechem's rape of Dinah, their sister and the daughter of Jacob and Leah. As a consequence, Jacob moved his family to Bethel. The Shechemites were also noted as members of a clan descended from Manasseh (Numbers 26.31).

Shilonites

Those who lived at or were associated with the shrine at Shiloh. The name is particularly applied to the priest Ahijah. Although Shiloh remained a holy place and place of holy associations, it was superseded by Jerusalem, the city to which David removed the ark.
(see Priests – Ahijah)

Shunammites

The inhabitants of Shunem, a town within the land allocated to Issachar (Joshua 19.17–19).

Diagram
Tribal Lands of Israel (8)

Sidonians

The principal Phoenician city-states were those of Tyre and Sidon. The Sidonians were the inhabitants of Sidon, although Phoenicians generally are referred to in the Bible as Sidonians. According to 1 Kings 11.1, Solomon included Sidonian women

in the 'many foreign women' he loved. The Sidonian, King Ethbaal was the father of Jezebel, the wife of Ahab (1 Kings 16.31). Ultimately, the Assyrians and the Babylonians respectively controlled the Phoenician states but they were largely restored to self-government by Persia, during which period they provided cedars for the rebuilding of the temple in Jerusalem.
(see *Phoenicians*)

Simeon, Tribe of

Simeon was the second son born to Jacob, and was the ancestor of the tribe of Simeon. 'She [Leah] conceived again and bore a son, and said, "Because the Lord has heard that I am hated, he has given me this son also"; and she named him Simeon' (Genesis 29.33). Their land allocation was south of the land given to Judah and was ultimately absorbed into Judah by the time of King David. Some families of the Simeonites pushed further south and took over lands occupied by the remnants of the Amalekites (1 Chronicles 4.24–43). (It does not seem that any Simeonites moved north to justify the tribe's association with the lost tribes of Israel – those who were deported from the land after the fall of Samaria in 721 BC.)

Diagrams
Children of Israel (3)
Tribal Lands of Israel (8)

Simon, Principal Individuals Named

There are five Simons noted under the *Friends, Relations and Acquaintances of Jesus* and two under the *People of the Acts of the Apostles*
(see also *Maccabees* and *People of the Acts of the Apostles*)

Sinites

One of the peoples who had descended from Canaan, the grandson of Noah (Genesis 10.15–17).

Sodomites

The inhabitants of the city of Sodom. Perhaps Sodom was representative of the ways of the neighbours of Abraham and his relations. In any event, the Lord had decided to make an example of Sodom (and indeed Gomorrah) and destroy it. He would first see for himself (Genesis 18.20,21). The two angels of the Lord ventured to the outskirts of Sodom where lived Abraham's brother, Lot. In accordance with the traditions of the Hebrews, he gave them hospitality – food and shelter for the night. Rowdy mobs encircled the dwelling during the evening 'and they called to Lot, "Where are the men who came to you tonight? Bring them out to us, so that we may know [in some translations 'abuse' is used rather than 'know'] them"' (Genesis 19.5).

In consequence of this story, sodomites are also those who commit the unnatural act envisaged in the text. (Such practices were an abhorrence and, therefore, forbidden (Leviticus 18.22).) The locations of Sodom and its companion city of Gomorrah are unknown, though educated speculation places them in an area on the south east coast of the Dead Sea.

Sumerians

The first people to create a significant and important civilization in Mesopotamia. They had settled around Ur by 3,400 BC; and by 3,000 BC, they boasted walled cities and a complex written language. From this area developed traditions of the Garden of Eden and of the Great Flood. A Semitic people had by this time established itself to the north and centred near Babylon in the city of Akkad. Towards the last quarter of this millennium, the influence of the Akkadians spread south and Sumeria came under their control, but the culture of the Sumerians was much respected by these people. However, by the end of the third millennium, the Sumerian supremacy at Ur was re-established following a destabilizing invasion of a number of races, including the Gutians, from the mountains of the north east. Eventually, Ur fell to waves of Elamites from the east in 1950 BC, and a period of instability followed with the influx of Hurrians from the north and Amorites from the south, until Sumeria was finally absorbed into the Amoritic Old Babylonian Empire (whose most illustrious king was Hammurabi (1728–1686 BC)), which, in turn, ended at the coming of the Hittites.

(see *Akkadians, Babylonians, Elamites, Hittites,* and *Hurrians*)

Diagram
Map of the Fertile Crescent (5)

Syrians

(see *Arameans*)

Ten Tribes of Israel or Lost Tribes of Israel

The tribes who were 'lost' or who were dispersed after the fall of Samaria in 722–721 BC at the hands of the Assyrian king, Sargon II. (Shalmaneser V had besieged Samaria for three years beforehand.)

'The king of Assyria carried the Israelites away to Assyria, settled them in Halah, on the Habor, the river of Gozan, and in the cities of the Medes' (2 Kings 18.11).

At the division of the kingdom, the ten tribes of the north, under Jeroboam, formed the northern kingdom of Israel. The tiny southern kingdom of Judah, under Rehoboam, the son of Solomon, comprised only the tribes of Judah and Benjamin. Probably, there were not ten tribes represented in the north. The Simeonites had settled south of Judah and, by the time of King David, had been largely absorbed by the tribe of Judah. Of course, not everyone had been taken away. In 2 Chronicles 34.9 contributions for the refurbishment of the temple at Jerusalem, during the reign of King Josiah of Judah, were made by members of the remnant of the tribes of Manasseh and Ephraim still living in the north.

(see *Samaritans, Simeon, Tribe of, Tribes of Israel*)

Diagram
Tribal Lands of Israel (8)

Thessalonians

The inhabitants of Thessalonica, a city situated in the north-west of the Thermaic Gulf. Cassander founded Thessalonica in 316 BC and named it after his wife.

Cassander was a general in the service of Alexander the Great. Two letters to the Thessalonians appear in the New Testament.
(see Letter Writers of the New Testament)

Twelve

The Twelve, generally speaking, refers to the twelve disciples (see *Disciples*) or the twelve apostles (see *Apostles*). It can also refer to the twelve tribes of Israel.
(see *Twelve Tribes of Israel*)

Twelve Tribes of Israel

These are the tribes who were the descendants of the twelve sons of Jacob (named Israel) and who took possession of Canaan following the Exodus from Egypt. However, no land was allocated to the tribe of Levi because it had been set aside for priestly duties, but the two sons of Joseph – Manasseh and Ephraim – were adopted by Jacob and they numbered among their uncles as ancestors of two of the tribes of Israel. The tribe of Joseph was, therefore, divided into the two tribes of Manasseh and Ephraim. Together, the twelve tribes of Israel were the Israelites.

From the time of the Israelites' entry into and conquest of Canaan, boundaries and borders changed frequently: some tribes increased their territory as others lost ground. The Simeonite land, for example, which was south of the land of Judah, had all but disappeared by the time of King David, having been absorbed by Judah. At the division of the two kingdoms, after the death of Solomon, the southern kingdom comprised only Judah and Benjamin.

(see *Children of Israel, Habiru, Hebrews, Patriarchs, Ten Tribes of Israel,* and the individual tribes.)

Diagrams
Descent of Abraham (1)
Family of Abraham (2)
Map of Canaan (6)

Wise Men of the Birth of Jesus

The wise men, the magi, or the astrologers, are the somewhat mysterious men who travelled some distance, probably from Mesopotamia, or beyond. Certainly their gifts came from farther afield. They had made their calculations from their study of the heavenly bodies, including their sighting of a new star (or, perhaps, it was Halley's Comet) and were led to believe that a new king had been born; someone of such importance that the risks involved in journeying into the Roman controlled Judea from lands well beyond Roman control, were worth taking. (Wise men – magi – had long been associated with Babylon, certainly since the Captivity.)

Matthew is the only evangelist to record the story. Its inclusion illustrates that from the very beginning the Christ was the Messiah not for Israel alone, but for the whole world. As the wise men, representing the Gentile world, knelt before him, Christ was revealed and made manifest to that world. The fear that Herod and the Jews felt at the news of the wise men's announcement, was the advance warning of the feeling most of the officials of the temple would have in due time towards Jesus' messiahship.

On account of the three named gifts we tend to assume that there were three wise men, but the Gospel does not tell us (Matthew 2).
(see *Family of Jesus – Jesus*)

Women at the Cross of Jesus and at the Tomb

There are clearly variations in the Gospel accounts, but they probably only reveal different recollections. Imagine that it was as though the different accounts relied upon snapshots of the gathering taken by various people placed at different vantage points. In one such snapshot, bystander 'A' might be abreast of the photographer and bystander 'B' unclear. In another, bystander 'C' might be in front of a little knot of people near the cross, and bystander 'A' nowhere to be seen. The accounts were obtained from a number of sources and traditions: it is small wonder that different memories recalled different people.

In Matthew's Gospel, the writer records that 'many women' (Matthew 27.55) had followed Jesus from Galilee and that they were observing the scene 'from a distance'. Among these women were Mary Magdalene, Mary the mother of James and Joseph, and the mother of Zebedee's sons (see *Brothers of Jesus*). At the tomb, the account records Mary Magdalene and 'the other Mary' (presumably, Mary, the mother of James and Joseph).

There were women, again, 'looking on from a distance' according to Mark, and they included 'Mary Magdalene, and Mary, the mother of James the younger and of Joses [Joseph] and Salome' [the mother of Zebedee's sons] (Mark 15.40). And these three women go to the tomb.

Luke tells us that 'all his acquaintances, including the women who had followed him from Galilee, stood at a distance, watching these things' (Luke 23.49). And it was these women who went to the tomb along with 'Mary Magdalene, Joanna, [and] Mary, the mother of James'. Some commentators suggest that Joanna and Salome are one and the same. Why should they be? Luke does not eliminate the possibility of Salome's presence by mentioning Joanna. The person of Joanna has not just been plucked out of the air; we meet her earlier in the Gospel as the wife of Chuza, Herod's steward, along with 'Susanna, and many others, who provided for them [Jesus and the disciples] out of their resources' (Luke 8.3). The inclusion of Joanna does not seem to be a slip of the pen!

John's Gospel concentrates on those nearest the cross during Jesus' final moments; and they are, in addition to the disciple whom Jesus loved (in all probability, John, the disciple, his cousin and son of Salome), Jesus' mother, his mother's sister (Salome), Mary the wife of Clopas, (the mother of James and Joseph) and Mary Magdalene. (John 19.25) (see *Brothers of Jesus*). Later, at the tomb, the writer is anxious to concentrate on the personal experiences of Mary Magdalene.

The picture one draws from the Gospels is of the cross in front of which stand Mary, Mother of Jesus, and John. At a distance, there is a small crowd of women and from that crowd Mary's sister (Salome), her sister-in-law (Mary, Wife of Clopas), and Mary Magdalene move forward to join John and Mary when the end draws near.

Diagrams
Family of John the Baptist (12)
Brothers of Jesus (13)

Writers of the New Testament

The New Testament comprises four Gospels, a sequel to one of the Gospels (the Acts of the Apostles), twenty-one letters, and a prophetic and apocalyptical work – the Revelation to John the Divine (also known as The Apocalypse). All twenty-seven books were written by AD 150 and largely accepted as scripture by the end of the fourth century AD.

For the writers of the Gospels see *Evangelists*; for the writer of Acts see *People of the Acts of the Apostles*; for the writers of the letters see *Letter Writers of the New Testament*.

Revelation (also known as The Apocalypse)

This extraordinary work gives us prophecy; messages to the seven churches – Ephesus, Smyrna, Pergamum, Thyatira, Sardis, Philadelphia and Laodicea – in the form of letters; an incredibly dramatic vision of heaven, past and present; and some profound theology. The aim of the book is to encourage the reader to see the world and its doings through heavenly eyes, and so gain a fresh perspective, a view from a different camera angle, as it were.

The writer of the Revelation was named John, a common enough name in the first century AD. There is no reason at all to associate this John with the apostle or with the writers of the Gospel of John and the letters of John. There is nothing known about the writer except that he wrote the book in exile on the Isle of Patmos, an island facing Asia and the seven churches to which the first four chapters of the book are aimed. It is believed that the book was written sometime during the last twenty years of the first century.

Writers of the Old Testament

The writers of the Bible are as much 'Bible People' as the characters featured within it, but the study of the composition, compilation and construction of the Old Testament is a complex matter indeed. Let us try to put it in a nutshell, though we may suffer from its over-simplification.

The creation of what we know as the Old Testament probably began in earnest during the stable period of Israel under Kings David and Solomon. There was a new national identity, indeed an *international* identity, because a loosely defined tribal confederacy with loosely defined tribal boundaries had become twelve administrative districts – twelve counties, if you like, answerable to the centre, to the crown. Tribal shrines and customs were largely discarded in favour of centralized worship concentrated on the temple in Jerusalem.

But Israel had a very long tradition of story-telling about the Creation, the Patriarchs, the Exodus, and so on (indeed, we know that by the time of Abraham's association with Ur, say, *c.* 1750 BC, the origins of the Noah's flood story and stories of the Garden of Eden were already about one thousand years old in that region): there were strands of stories with different emphases from the north and from the south. Would they be lost forever? They were not, because against the background of the stable monarchy, literary and theological talents could flourish and begin the work of assembling the histories and beliefs as they had been handed down to that point. These traditions stretching back to Moses and beyond, embraced not only oral tradition but written work as well – including law codes and, probably, the songs of Miriam and Deborah (Exodus 15.1–18 and Judges 5). During the tenth century BC, this work was undertaken from the southern perspective, if you like, and in the ninth century BC, a collection of oral traditions was assembled reflecting the northern slant. Late in the eighth century BC, these two strands were drawn together.

In the seventh century BC, the discovery of the core of Deuteronomy in the temple was the impetus for King Josiah's reform. About this time the chapters 17–26 of Leviticus were reworked.

The priestly editors of the Exile and the Return drew all this work together to form the Pentateuch – Genesis, Exodus, Leviticus, Numbers and Deuteronomy.

The written sources for the books of Samuel and the books of Kings were preserved in the annals of Judah and Israel and these were edited and extended with the earlier traditions of the judges period to create the books of the Former Prophets – Joshua, Judges, 1 and 2 Samuel, and 1 and 2 Kings – during the Exile in Babylon. The Latter Prophets – Isaiah, Jeremiah, Ezekiel, and Hosea to Malachi – were collected and edited by the prophets' various disciples and scribes from the eighth century BC to the fourth century BC. The final group of books, The Writings – Job, Psalms, Proverbs, Canticles (various), Ruth, Lamentations, Ecclesiastes, Esther, Daniel, Ezra, Nehemiah, and 1 and 2 Chronicles – date from the tenth century BC and before (in the case of some of the psalms and canticles) to Lamentations in the sixth century BC and to Esther and Daniel late in the third century BC or early in the second. 1 and 2 Chronicles almost parallel 1 and 2 Kings in their history of the southern kingdom: the sources for Chronicles were, therefore, those used for Kings.

This, then, is the Jewish bible, which, incidentally, was translated into Greek, during the third century BC, by scholars in Alexandria, and known as the Septuagint. More correctly, it should be known as the Alexandrian version. The story that seventy-two scholars (rounded to seventy!) – six from each of the twelve tribes of Israel – were invited to travel from Palestine to Egypt in order to undertake this work is unlikely to be true. Most scholars agree that the Greek used is clearly the language of Alexandria during the Ptolomaic period. The Septuagint contains additional books, which are included in modern Bibles as part of the Old Testament, or in the Apocrypha.

Genesis

Concerned with the origins of the world and of life itself, with particular reference to the descent from Adam, the Great Flood, the descent from Noah, the covenant God made with Abraham (Genesis 17.1–8), and the saga of Abraham's descendants and their arrival in Egypt.

Exodus

Tells the story of the Exodus, of Moses and Aaron, and the escape to the wilderness. The second half of the book is concerned with the laws for a secure social structure, and the consecration of priests and the making of suitable vestments.

Leviticus

Wholly concerned with ritual notes for the levitical priesthood.

Numbers

Certainly contains plenty of figures and statistics. It also contains more law, and traces the Israelites from Sinai, through the desert to their first steps in Canaan.

Writers of the Old Testament

Deuteronomy
Completes the Pentateuch cycle and ends with the death of Moses. Deuteronomy contains the 'new' or, rather, 'second' law made to replace the law contained in Exodus 20.22–23.19.

Joshua
Traces the campaigns of Joshua in Canaan until his death, and sets out the land allocation for the tribes of Israel.

Judges
The story of the Israelites campaigning against the peoples of Canaan and also trying to live alongside them. The series of stories highlights episodes in the careers of notable chieftains, or judges.

Ruth
A short story about faithfulness based in an historical context and, it is reasonable to suppose, founded on a true episode.

1 and 2 Samuel (1 and 2 Kings)
Takes us from the end of the period of the judges with the birth of Samuel, part prophet, part priest, part judge, through the rise of the monarchy and the conflict between Saul and David, to the last days of David.

1 and 2 Kings (3 and 4 Kings)
Traces the decline of Israel's faithfulness to God. They trace the monarchy from Solomon to the division of the kingdom through the parallel histories of the separate monarchies to the destruction of the northern kingdom of Israel by Assyria, to the defeat of the southern kingdom of Judah by Babylon. (The writers here are concerned with showing how, through the evidence of their history, the two kingdoms ended their days in exile both from their lands and from God.) The prophets Elijah and Elisha are both featured in the first book; Elisha in the second.

1 and 2 Chronicles
Deals with the reigns of David and Solomon, and then the kings of the southern kingdom.

Ezra and Nehemiah (1 Esdras and 2 Esdras)
Many believe that the writer of 1 and 2 Chronicles was also responsible in some way – as the writer or as the collector – for the texts of Ezra and Nehemiah. These books deal with Cyrus' decree and the subsequent return to Jerusalem and settlement of those taken into Captivity in Babylon by Nebuchadnezzar.

Tobit (Tobias)
Included in the Apocrypha of some versions of the Bible. A gentle moral tale about God. Whether or not it is a fictional tale or based on real events is impossible to determine. It may have been written in about 200 BC.

Judith

Included in the Apocrypha of some versions of the Bible. A story about the vastness of God acting through the woman, Judith. It was written, in all probability, after the beginning of the second century BC.

Esther

The conclusion of this story, added by a Greek translator of the first part, appears in the Apocrypha of some versions of the Bible.

Probably a story based upon real events in the fifth century BC.
(see *Kings of Other Lands – Xerxes*)

1 and 2 Maccabees

Included in the Apocrypha in some versions of the Bible.

The first book is an historical account of the Maccabees but both books aim to instruct the reader about the need for purity of faith and recognition of the law.

Job

A book of obscure and complex structure. It is concerned with the problem of suffering and the mystery of the purposes of God. The work probably dates from after the Return.

Psalms

A collection of hymns and poems drawn from centuries of the worship of God. The book is set out in five parts: 1–41; 42–72; 73–89; 90–106; 107–150.

Proverbs

A collection of poetry and sayings from the time of Solomon and edited during the time of the exile in Babylon.

Ecclesiastes

Perhaps this book was intended to elicit from the listener a positive reaction to the rather narrow and sceptical viewpoints expressed. It is thought to date from around 250 BC.

Song of Solomon (Song of Songs/Canticle of Canticles)

A group of poems about love collected during the exile. Some may have been of considerable antiquity even then. Although the poems are concerned with sexual attraction and love, Christians have used them as a metaphor for Christ's love for his Church.

The Wisdom of Solomon (The Book of Wisdom)

Included in the Apocrypha in some versions of the Bible.

The original language of this book was Greek and was composed in Alexandria sometime after the translation of the Septuagint. This profound book is aimed at strengthening faith and encouraging philosophical enquiry.

Sirach (Ecclesiasticus)

Included in the Apocrypha in some versions of the Bible.

In form it is a rather muddled collection of notes, lectures, hymns and prayers accumulated over the years by the author, Ben Sira.

Isaiah and Jeremiah
(see *Prophets – Isaiah I, II and III and Jeremiah*)

Lamentations
Five beautiful laments over Jerusalem after the first wave of deportations to Babylon had occurred. The message is that despite what has happened, God is still with his people, and his merciful kindness has not diminished. It was thought at one time that the author of Lamentations was Jeremiah the prophet. Scholars now believe this unlikely.

Baruch (Baruch/The Letter of Jeremiah)
Included in the Apocrypha of some versions of the Bible.

The book comprises a rather confused collection of short items probably dating from more than two hundred years after the captivity and return.

Ezekiel, Daniel, Hosea, Joel, Amos, Obadiah, Jonah, Micah, Nahum, Habakkuk, Zephaniah, Haggai, Zechariah and Malachi
(see *Prophets – Ezekiel to Malachi*)

3 and 4 Esdras
Included only in the Apocrypha of some versions of the Bible.

The first of these books parallels Ezra and a portion of 2 Chronicles. Only two chapters are unique to the book. The bulk of the second book dates from about the destruction of the temple in AD 70.

The Prayer of Manasseh
Included only in the Apocrypha of some versions of the Bible.

This was probably written sometime after the Septuagint in Alexandria. It is a prayer of penitence.

3 and 4 Maccabees
Included only in the Apocrypha of some versions of the Bible.

The first book bears no relation to the Maccabean revolt or to the Maccabean dynasty. The second was written, probably, in memory of the Maccabeans in Antioch sometime before AD 70.

Zealots

The Zealots were so named because they were zealous for Israel. They were an extreme party whose aim was the overthrow and expulsion of the Roman invader and occupier. It seems that Simon the Zealot, one of the twelve disciples of Jesus, had been one of them.
(see *Disciples of Jesus*)

Zebulun, Tribe of

Zebulun was Jacob's tenth son and Leah's sixth. 'Then Leah said, "God has endowed me with a good dowry; now my husband will honour me, because I have borne him six sons"; so she named him Zebulun' (Genesis 30.20). He was the ancestor of the tribe of Zebulun, whose land lay south west of Galilee between the lands of

Manasseh and Issachar to the south and those of Asher and Naphtali to the north (Joshua 19.10).

Diagrams
Children of Israel (3)
Tribal Lands of Israel (8)

Appendix

Diagrams

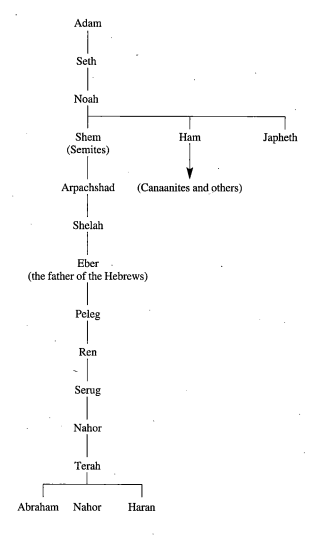

1. Descent of Abraham

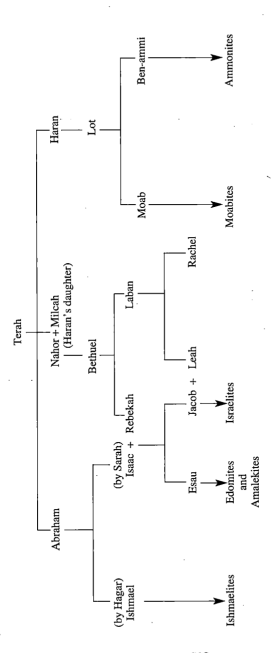

2. Family of Abraham

113

Appendix

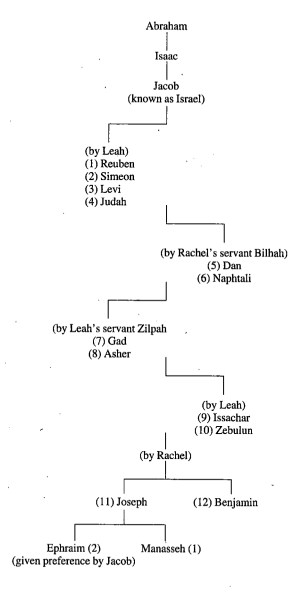

3. Children (the sons) of Israel

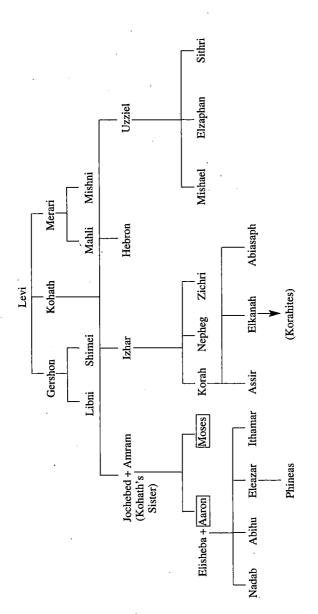

4. Tree of the Tribe of Levi

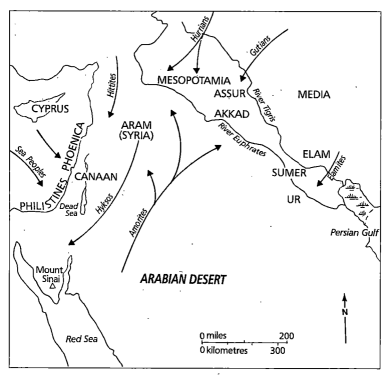

5. Map of the Fertile Crescent

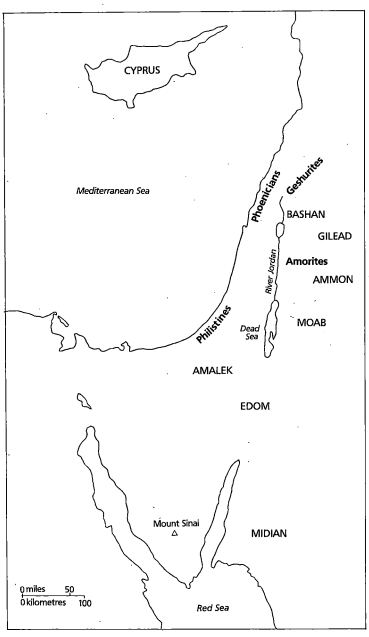

6. Map of Canaan

117

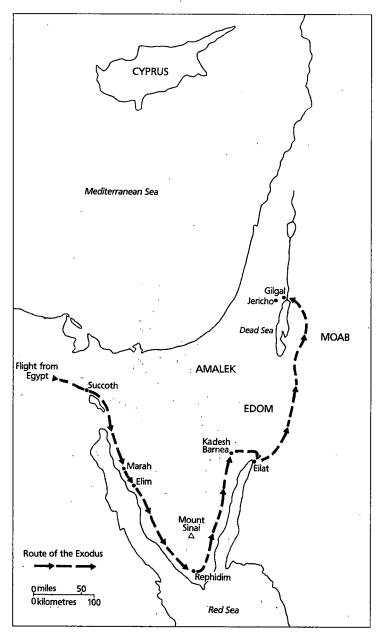

7. The Route of the Exodus

118

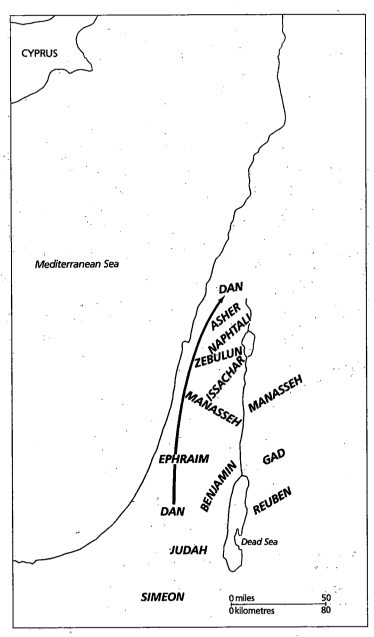

CYPRUS

Mediterranean Sea

DAN

ASHER

NAPHTALI

ZEBULUN

ISSACHAR

MANASSEH

MANASSEH

EPHRAIM

GAD

BENJAMIN

DAN

REUBEN

Dead Sea

JUDAH

SIMEON

0 miles 50
0 kilometres 80

8. Tribal Lands of Israel

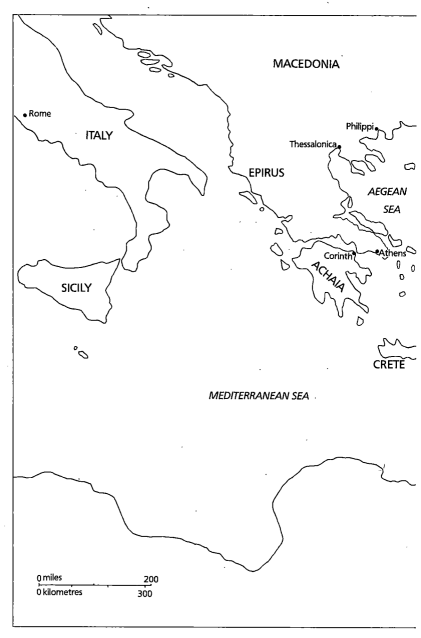

9. The Mediterranean in the First Century AD

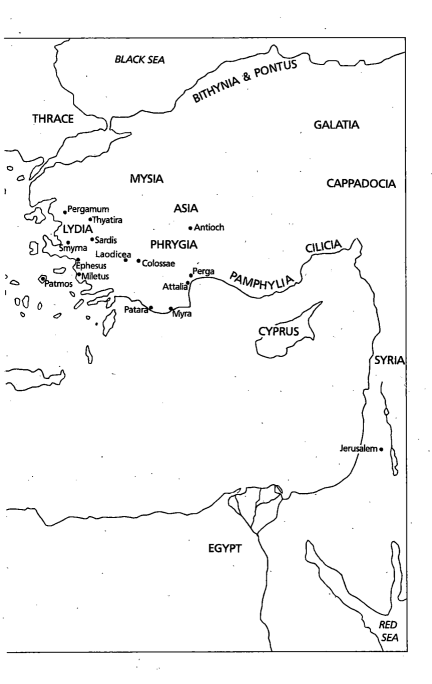

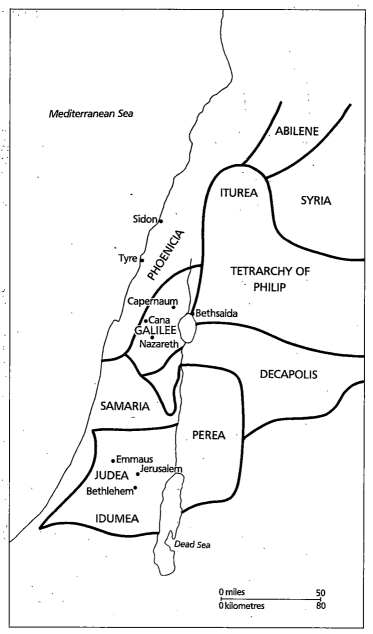

10. The Holy Land in the First Century AD

122

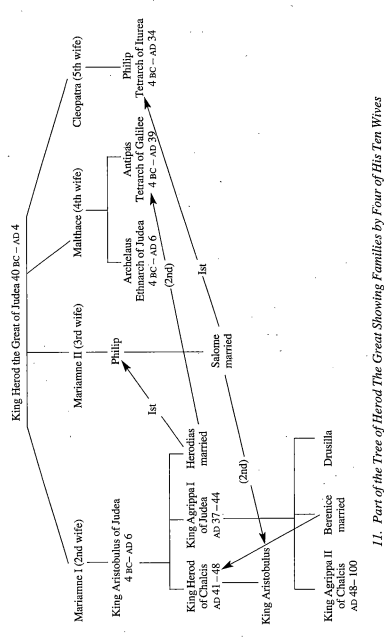

11. Part of the Tree of Herod The Great Showing Families by Four of His Ten Wives

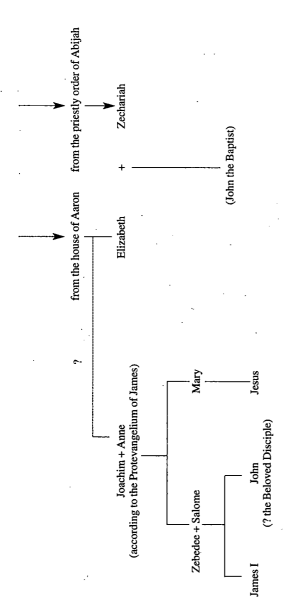

12. Family of John the Baptist

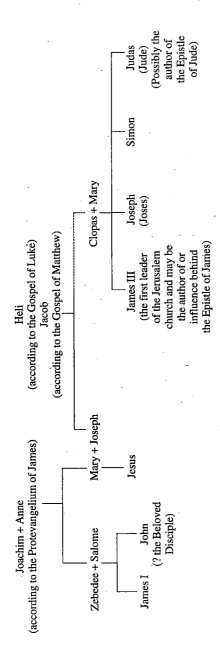

13. Brothers of Jesus

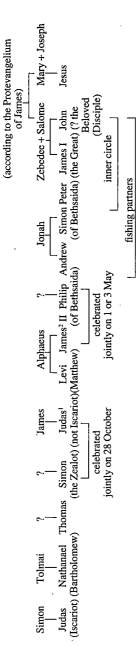

Joachim + Anne
(according to the Protevangelium
of James)

Mary + Joseph — Jesus

Zebedee + Salome: James I (the Great), John (? the Beloved Disciple) — inner circle

Jonah: Simon Peter (of Bethsaida), Andrew — fishing partners

Alphaeus: Levi (Matthew), James² II, Philip (of Bethsaida) — celebrated jointly on 1 or 3 May

James, Judas¹ (not Iscariot), Simon (the Zealot), ? — celebrated jointly on 28 October

Thomas, ?

Tolmai, Nathanael (Bartholomew)

Simon, Judas (Iscariot)

1 Sometimes confused with Judas, the author of the Epistle of Jude
2 Sometimes confused with James III

14. Disciples of Jesus

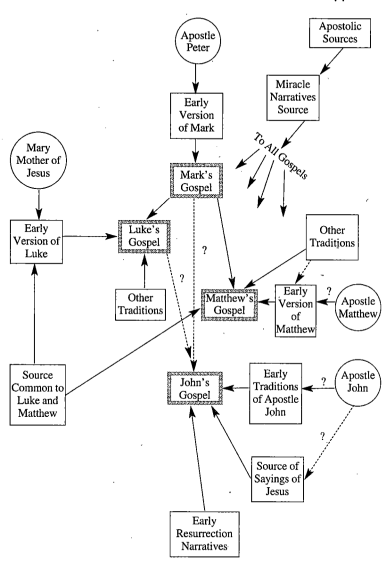

15. Evangelists and Their Sources

Appendix

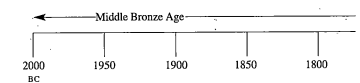

2000 BC	1950	1900	1850	1800

Patriarchs/
Hebrews/
Israelites

Palestine   under Egyptian control
and Religion

Egypt   12th–18th Dynasties, during which Egypt suffered the Hyksos

Mesopotamia Amorite Invasions ⟶ 1st Babylonian Era
and Region

16. Broad Outline of Parallel Histories

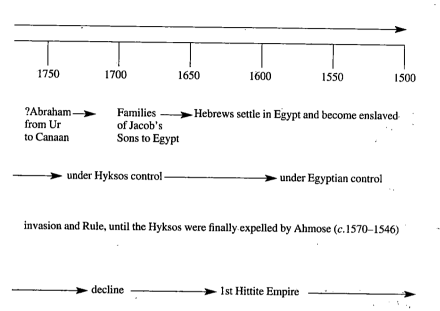

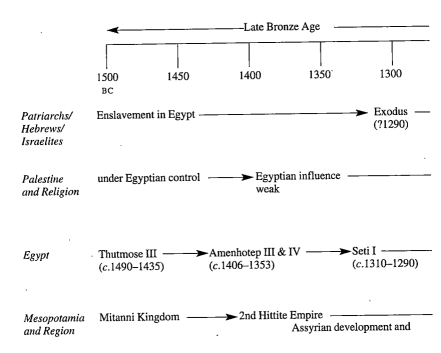

17. Broad Outline of Parallel Histories

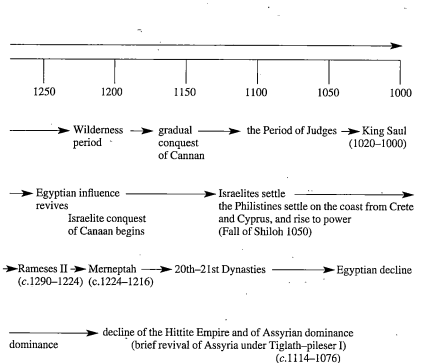

1250   1200   1150   1100   1050   1000

⟶ Wilderness ⟶ gradual ⟶ the Period of Judges ⟶ King Saul
period   conquest   (1020–1000)
               of Cannan

⟶ Egyptian influence ⟶ Israelites settle
revives   the Philistines settle on the coast from Crete
     Israelite conquest   and Cyprus, and rise to power
     of Canaan begins   (Fall of Shiloh 1050)

⟶Rameses II ⟶ Merneptah ⟶ 20th–21st Dynasties ⟶ Egyptian decline
(*c.*1290–1224) (*c.*1224–1216)

⟶ decline of the Hittite Empire and of Assyrian dominance
dominance   (brief revival of Assyria under Tiglath–pileser I)
                      (*c.*1114–1076)

Appendix

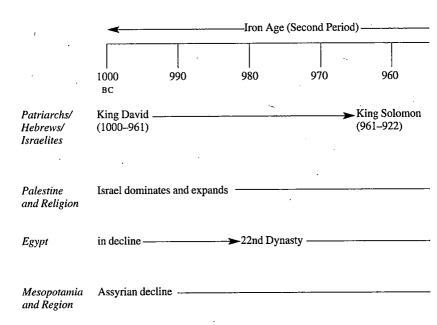

18. Broad Outline of Parallel Histories

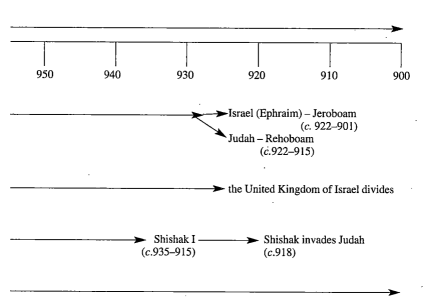

950   940   930   920   910   900

Israel (Ephraim) – Jeroboam
(*c.* 922–901)
Judah – Rehoboam
(*c.*922–915)

the United Kingdom of Israel divides

Shishak I ——→ Shishak invades Judah
(*c.*935–915)   (*c.*918)

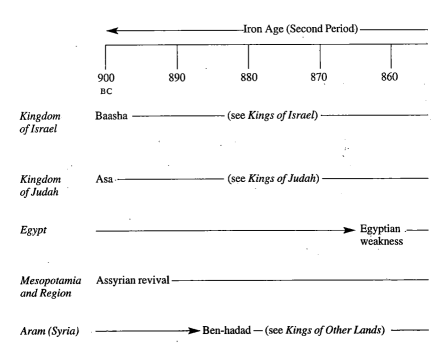

19. Broad Outline of Parallel Histories

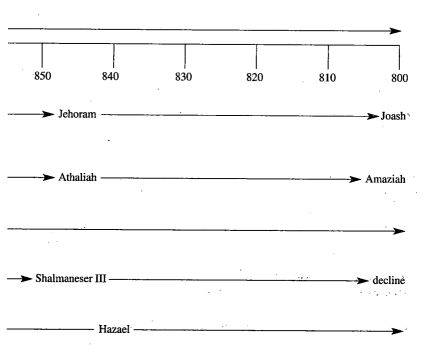

Appendix

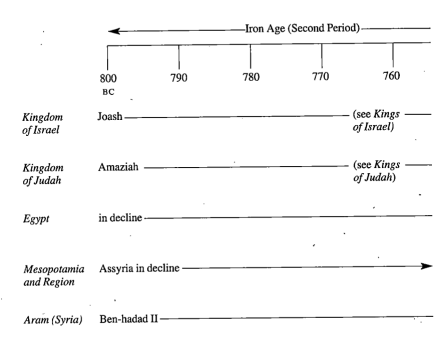

20. Broad Outline of Parallel Histories

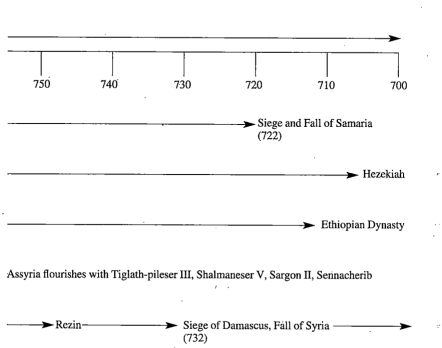

750   740   730   720   710   700

Siege and Fall of Samaria (722)

Hezekiah

Ethiopian Dynasty

Assyria flourishes with Tiglath-pileser III, Shalmaneser V, Sargon II, Sennacherib

Rezin — Siege of Damascus, Fall of Syria (732)

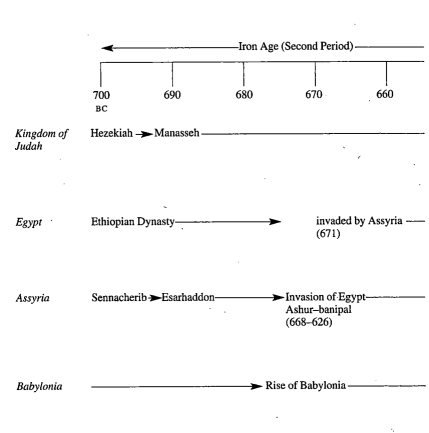

21. Broad Outline of Parallel Histories

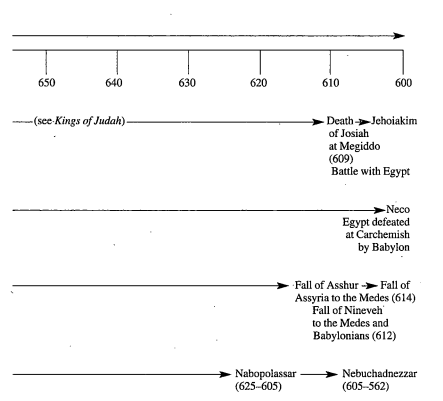

Appendix

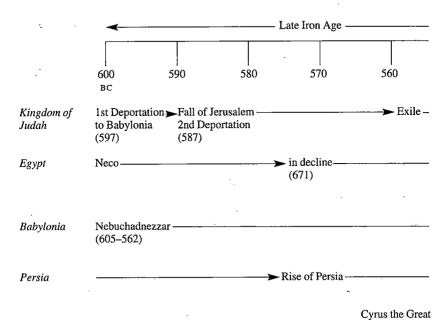

22. Broad Outline of Parallel Histories

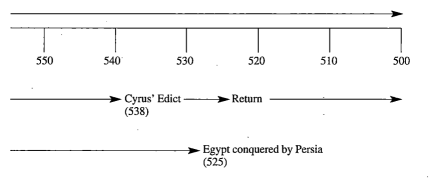

Cyrus' Edict ──────► Return ───────────────────►
(538)

Egypt conquered by Persia
(525)

──►Nabonidus ─────► Fall of Babylon to Persia
(555–539)   (539)

──► Defeat of ───────────────► Cambyses ──► Darius I
the Medes   (530–522)   (522–)
(550)
Conquest of Babylon (539)

Further Reading

B. W. Anderson, *The Living World of the Old Testament*, Longmans, 1964

John Barton and John Muddiman (eds), *The Oxford Bible Commentary*, Oxford University Press, 2001

M. Black and H. H. Rowley (eds), *Peake's Commentary on the Bible*, Thomas Nelson, 1963

Raymond E. Brown, Joseph A. Fitzmyer and Roland E. Murphy (eds), *The New Jerome Bible Handbook*, The Liturgical Press, 1993

Cruden's Complete Concordance of the Bible, Lutterworth, 1977

Freedman (ed.), *Eerdmans Dictionary of the Bible*, William B. Eerdmans, 2000

C. Grant and H. H. Rowley (eds), *Dictionary of the Bible*, T and T Clark, 1963

A. Kamm, *The Israelites*, Routledge, 1999

H. S. Kee and F. W. Young, *The Living World of the New Testament*, DLT, 1962

P. J. King and L. E. Stager, *Life in Biblical Israel*, Westminster John Knox Press, 2002

Herbert G. May and Bruce M. Metzger (eds), *The New Oxford Annotated Bible*, Oxford University Press, 1971

Dom Bernard Orchard MA (Cantab) and Revd Edmund F. Sutcliffe SJ MA (Oxon) (eds), *A Catholic Commentary on Holy Scripture*, Thomas Nelson, 1953

John Rogerson (ed.), *The Oxford Illustrated History of the Bible*, Oxford University Press, 2001

The Septuagint, S. Bagster and Sons Ltd (year of publication not known)